To Bob,
Looking forward
to hearing
your story!
Fran and Tom Tourle

The first
husband-and-wife team
to circumnavigate
the world.

The first pilot
to navigate
around the world
using GPS.

FLYING TOGETHER AROUND THE WORLD

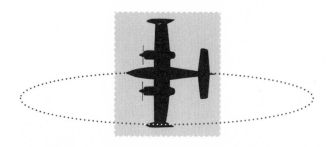

Tom and Fran Towle

TWIN AIR PUBLICATIONS
MIAMI

Twin Air Publications
80 S.W. 17th Road
Miami, Florida 33129
305-858-6777

Twin Air Publications and colophon are
registered trademarks of Twin Air Services, Inc.

An Andrew Rock book
Designed by Chris Lloyd, DDS Designs
Typography by WordSmiths, Inc.
Manufactured in the United States of America

Library of Congress Cataloging-in-Publication Data
Towle, Tom, 1939–
    Flying together around the world / Tom and Fran Towle.
        p. cm.
    ISBN 0-9634095-9-X : $16.95
    1. Towle, Tom, 1939– . 2. Towle, Fran, 1943– . 3. Flights around
the world. 4. Global Positioning System. I. Towle, Fran, 1943– .
II. Title.
G445.T66 1993
910.4'1--dc20   92-37699
                                                                CIP

Portions of *Flying Together Around the World* have appeared
previously in slightly different forms in *AOPA Pilot*,
The Twin Cessna Flyer, *GPS World*, *Plane Pilot*, and
The Aviation Consumer.

TO OUR PARENTS

N76TT's 28,587-mile Flight

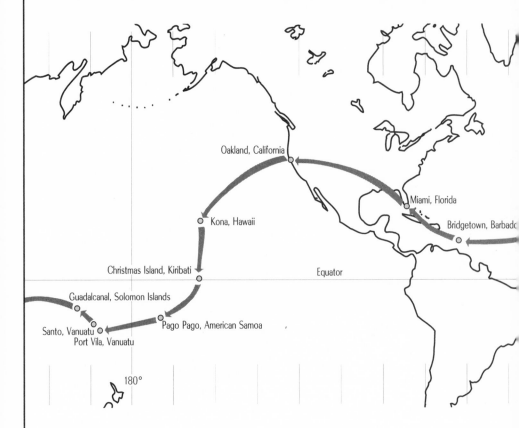

Identifier	Location	Latitude	Longitude
KOAK	Oakland, California, U.S.A.	37°43.35'N	122°13.29'W
PHKO	Kona, Hawaii, U.S.A.	19°44.18'N	156°03.84'W
PLCH	Christmas Island, Kiribati	01°59.21'N	157°22.03'W
NSTU	Pago, Pago, American Samoa	14°20.68'S	170°43.72'W
NVVV	Port Vila, Vanuatu	17°42.93'S	168°19.17'E
NVSS	Santo, Vanuatu	15°31.61'S	167°13.44'E
AGGH	Guadalcanal, Solomon Islands	09°25.25'S	160°03.19'E
ADDN	Darwin, Australia	12°25.82'S	130°53.62E
WRRR	Bali, Indonesia	08°45.43'S	115°10.10'E
WSSL	Singapore, Malaysia	01°25.77'N	103°52.38'E

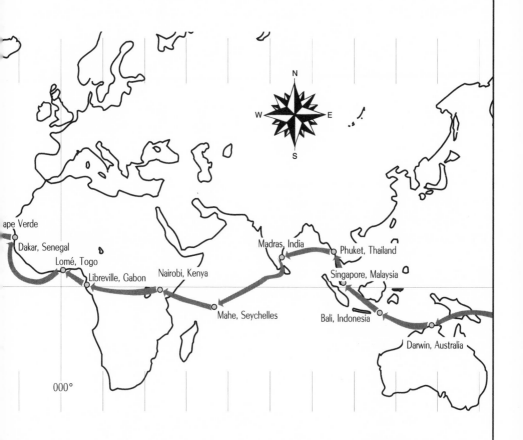

Identifier	Location	Latitude	Longitude
VTSP	Phuket, Thailand	08°07.91'N	098°19.76'E
VOMM	Madras, India	13°00.12'N	080°11.87'E
FSSS	Mahe, Seychelles	04°40.63'S	055°31.28'E
HKNW	Nairobi, Kenya	01°19.71'S	036°49.99'E
FOOL	Libreville, Gabon	00°27.00'N	009°25.11'E
DXXX	Lomé, Togo	06°10.08'N	001°15.75'E
GOOY	Dakar, Senegal	14°45.51'N	017°30.45'W
GVAC	Sal, Cape Verde	16°45.22'N	022°57.10'W
TBPB	Bridgetown, Barbados	13°03.87'N	059°28.97'W
KMIA	Miami, Florida, U.S.A.	25°47.78'N	080°17.12'W

CESSNA 310R

HEIGHT .... 10' 11.8"
LENGTH .... 31' 11.5"
WINGSPAN .... 36' 11"

2 SIX-CYLINDER FUEL-INJECTED 285-H.P. CONTINENTAL ENGINES
2 CONSTANT-SPEED THREE-BLADE MCCAULEY PROPELLERS

SURVIVAL GEAR

1 FOUR-MAN LIFE RAFT WITH SURVIVAL EQUIPMENT AND CANOPY
1 HIGH-QUALITY WATER DESALINIZATION UNIT
2 LIFE JACKETS WITH LIGHTS
1 NOAA EXPERIMENTAL MINIATURE EMERGENCY POSITION INDICATING RADIO
   BEACON; COSPAS-SARSAT SEARCH AND RESCUE SATELLITE SYSTEM
2 HAND-HELD EMERGENCY LOCATOR TRANSMITTERS
1 HAND-HELD VHF TRANSCEIVER AND BATTERY PACKS

FUEL TANK PLACEMENT

STANDARD FUEL TANK LOCATIONS   * ADDED FUEL TANK LOCATIONS

STANDARD	ADDED
50	80
10	80
20	80
20	20
10	260
50	
160	

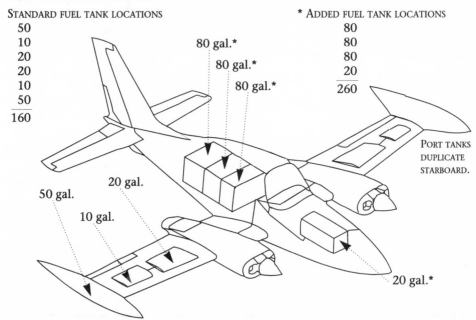

80 gal.*
80 gal.*
80 gal.*

PORT TANKS
DUPLICATE
STARBOARD.

20 gal.

50 gal.

10 gal.

20 gal.*

ELECTRONICS

Dual King KX155 NAV COM Transceivers
Dual King Glideslope Receivers
Dual Head ARC ADF Receivers
King ADF Receiver
Marker Beacon Receiver
DME Transceiver
Emergency Locator Transmitter
Transponder Transceiver
Bendix Radar
HF Transceiver, mounted between pilot and copilot seats with
    power unit in nose compartment. Antenna connected to power
    unit and extended from nose to tip of vertical tail.
GPS-TNL-2000 Navigator Receiver, permanently panel-mounted
GPS-Portable TransPak Receiver positioned on glareshield.
    (Both GPS receivers could be connected to one external GPS antenna.)

PERFORMANCE

	STANDARD	MODIFIED
Maximum Takeoff Weight	5,500 lbs.	6,875 lbs.
Maximum Landing Weight	5,400 lbs.	5,400 lbs.
Empty Weight	3,575 lbs.	3,680 lbs.
Useful Load	1,925 lbs.	3,195 lbs.

STANDARD	MODIFIED
Fuel .... 160 gallons (usable)	420 gallons

Nose compartment 20 gallons
Cabin behind front seats 240 gallons
in 3 steel rectangular tanks
80 gal. ea. (gravity fed)

Range ...... 1,152 nautical miles	384.4 gallons (usable)
6.5 hours	16 hours @ 24 gph

Prologue

"N76TT, turn immediately to two-seven-zero degrees! You are in a prohibited danger zone!"

Twelve thousand miles from home, our twin-engine Cessna 310 droned smoothly through the skies above Sri Lanka, a primitive island-nation off the southern tip of India. Suddenly, the radio came alive with an agitated voice.

"Aircraft calling Colombo Control, what is the nature of your emergency? What is the emergency? Report your position immediately!"

I squeezed the microphone button. "Roger, Colombo Control, this is Cessna November-Seven-Six-Tango-Tango. There is no emergency. We've been handed off to you from Madras Control."

"November-Seven-Six-Tango-Tango, state your emergency and Air Force identification."

"Negative, negative, Colombo, we are a non-military aircraft on Airway Alpha four-six-five proceeding to Dabar fix."

"November-Seven-Six-Tango-Tango, turn immediately to two-seven-zero degrees! You are in a prohibited danger zone! Turn to two-seven-zero degrees. State your commander's name, country, and postal address."

An international incident! Halfway around the world, I had apparently misread an obscure Sri Lankan regulation and was directly over the combat zone of the thousand-year religious war between the Tamils and the Sinhalese, which had flared up recently in the northern part of the island. How did I ever get Fran and myself into such a predicament, anyway?

1

> **"**...it seemed as if I was born
> with a natural desire to fly
> just a little further,
> to see what lies over the next hill.**"**

A yellow Piper Cub instilled in me at age five a permanent lust to fly, to soar among the clouds in my own plane. I started taking flying lessons in a Cub at age 17, and I still have a crystal-clear memory of my first flight, a 30-minute hop from a short grass strip at Nedrow Airpark near Syracuse, New York. Coming in for a landing, the instructor let me have the controls, and by sheer luck I gently skimmed the wheels onto the grass in a perfect, whisper-soft three-point landing — a feat I still have difficulty duplicating in a tail dragger.

After my first solo flight, my instructor warned me not to fly more than 25 miles from the airport until I got checked out for cross-country flight. As I made my local practice flights, I chafed under that 25-mile restriction; it seemed as if I was born with a natural desire to fly just a little farther, to see what lies over the next hill. I went on to earn my pilot's license, and in 1972 bought an Ercoupe, a little two-seater with a canopy that can slide open in flight. Cruising along at 110 mph with our hair blowing in the wind, my wife Fran and I explored the airports near our home in the Miami area, and then ventured out to many of the islands in the

Bahamas, and even up to the Carolinas. Always I dreamed of flying just a little further.

As our family grew, we moved up to a four-seat Mooney M-20G, and then to a twin-engine Piper Apache. That portly, under-powered aircraft took us further than ever—to California, Oregon, and Washington state. Each cross-country flight was an escape from earthbound stress and hustle, and each whetted my appetite to fly further and further from Miami. I sold the Apache in 1982, and began building a fund to buy the one airplane I felt could do it all: a Cessna 310, a sleek twin-engine six-passenger craft that can cruise at well over 200 mph and fly 1,300 miles nonstop. On April 25, 1986, Fran and I gave each other a 16th wedding anniversary present: a 1976 model Cessna 310R. Its registration number and call sign was November-Seven-Six-Tango-Tango.

That first summer, we took N76TT to Newfoundland. Passing over the Canadian border into a different country gave me a renewed sense of excitement and adventure. When we reached St. John's, a town on the eastern tip of Newfoundland, a traditional jumping-off spot for trans-Atlantic flights in small aircraft, "it" happened. The day was glorious, the sun and sea dazzled my imagination. I tried to comprehend what it was like for Lindbergh and all the trans-Atlantic flyers who followed him—to keep flying out over that vast ocean instead of meekly doing a 180-degree turn and heading back to familiar territory. Crossing the Atlantic would be a large and serious undertaking, more than just putting "E" for Europe in the compass window and waiting for landfall. Before we got back to Miami, the idea began to percolate in my mind for a flight to Europe with the whole family, which by now included Tiffany, 13; Tom III, 11; and Michael, 4.

4

For years, Tom had been talking about a flight around the world. He was obviously eager to go, and since I'd been his loyal "copilot" on so many previous trips, I sure wasn't going to let him leave me behind for the big one. But our children were very young and I didn't feel right about leaving them for an extended period of time. A mother just doesn't leave her 4-year-old for two months.

I encouraged Tom to plan a European trip. We could make it without extra fuel tanks in the cabin, so there would be room for the whole family to come along. We'd still have the adventure of making a long flight over the ocean and landing in several remote and exotic countries.

After our return to Florida, we began to plan a flight to Italy, where Fran's sister lives with her Italian husband, an oil-rig helicopter pilot. Our route would take us north of the Arctic Circle, over a brutally cold ocean filled with icebergs. Even the land we would be flying over—northern Canada, Greenland, and Iceland—would be frigid and foreboding. Small planes are routinely flown nonstop across the Atlantic by professional ferry pilots who temporarily install long-range auxiliary fuel tanks in the cabin. Because we would have five occupants in N76TT, there would be no room for ferry tanks; however, there were several other details to be resolved.

I ordered the *International Flight Information Manual* from the U.S. Department of Transportation's Federal Aviation Administration [FAA]. This manual is a preflight and planning guide for aviators flying outside the United States. It contains foreign entry requirements, a directory of aerodromes of entry, and pertinent regulations and restrictions. Since information is always subject to change, it is a pilot's responsibility to obtain the latest data from other sources as well. A pilot assumes all responsibility for his plane, including avoiding all danger areas and restricted areas. A pilot must comply with all requirements and regulations of each territory. All countries require some form of advance notification of arrival. Some countries make it easier than others for pilots. I've come to enjoy planning international flights.

On July 28, 1987, after a surprise interview for Miami's WSVN-TV7 News and bidding farewell to friends and relatives, we took off from Miami for Goose Bay, Labrador, the first stepping stone on our great-circle route. Ten minutes after takeoff, a back-seat teen-age skirmish erupted, and Michael chimed in wanting to know if we were there yet. Things soon calmed down, however, and we got "there" after 12 hours of flying and two refueling stops.

At Goose Bay, we wearily checked into the Labrador Inn in the little town of Happy Valley, and the next morning I walked the three miles to the weather station to get the latest briefing about conditions in Narsarsuaq, Greenland, the next stop on our hopscotch great-circle route to Italy.

"How would you like to fly with me to Narsarsuaq in my little 310 today?" I asked the meteorologist. (I found this was a good way to get a forecaster's true feelings about the weather.)

"Not today," he replied. Narsarsuaq, nestled at the bottom of a deep fjord, was shrouded in fog.

For three days we repeated this ritual; Narsarsuaq remained fogbound. On the fourth day, the meteorologist advised that if we took off right away the weather would probably be good at Søndrestrøm, a Danish Air Force base on the western coast of Greenland hundreds of miles north of our intended course. Although it was a bit of a detour, I decided to go for it.

We took off hurriedly, leaving North America behind. As the hours passed, the ice-blue ocean turned white with foam, and huge icebergs dotted the seas. Some of them appeared to be more than a mile square, and might serve as emergency landing spots. Our two 285-hp Continental engines hummed along at 2300 rpm and 22 inches of manifold pressure, a 58% power setting that gave the best overall compromise of speed, range, and fuel consumption.

As we approached the desolate, wintry, mountainous coast of Greenland, I realized we were committed to land at Søndrestrøm, for we had only 45 minutes of fuel remaining and there was no alternate airport within range. If Søndrestrøm were fogged in, we could be in serious trouble. (On the brighter side, the ice that had been forming on the wings and windshield had mostly disappeared.) When I called Søndrestrøm, they reported four miles visibility and an 800-foot ceiling with light snow. Not exactly sunbathing weather, but certainly good enough for us to make a routine instrument landing. A mile from the airfield—30 seconds before touchdown—I still couldn't make out the runway. As if camouflaged, it blended in with the terrain. It had to be there! My instruments told me it was there. Finally, the runway's outline popped into view and we made a smooth landing.

As we were rolling out on the runway, the right engine quit. No problem, I said to myself, just a minor glitch; we'll crank it up and taxi over to the customs area. Despite my best efforts, the engine would not restart. We taxied on the left engine alone to the parking area and tried again to restart the right. No luck.

This could be disastrous. A major mechanical problem could ground us in Greenland for days or weeks. I decided to complete the customs formalities and refuel the plane before investigating the engine further. We paid $168 in processing fees, plus a $100 fine for making a landing without prior written authorization, and an astounding $1,200 for fuel (138 gallons at nearly $9 per gallon).

I was told there were no mechanics around, but that in a few days it might be possible to borrow one from the Danish Air Force. If engine parts were needed, they could be shipped from the U.S. to Copenhagen, where they could be put aboard the chartered DC-8 that flew in supplies to Søndrestrøm once a week. I had visions of our family being stranded here for the rest of the summer.

I walked across the tarmac to N76TT and tried one more time to start the right engine. It came alive! Truly wonderful, but not totally satisfying from the standpoints of safety and reliability. One-time and intermittent problems are always the most difficult to diagnose. Trying to duplicate the problem, I ran the engine at various power and magneto settings; perfect from idle to full power. I removed the engine cowling and carefully inspected all the fuel hoses and electrical connections; no leaks, all wiring intact and secure. After shaking the wings up and down, I drained more than a gallon of fuel from the tanks and sumps; not a drop of water showed. If an engine is getting proper fuel and ignition it must run; oversimplified, but true. There was nothing left to verify.

To get out of the cold, Fran and the kids boarded the plane while I ran to get the weather forecast and file the flight plan for the next leg to Reykjavik, Iceland. Taxiing out, I was uneasy at the prospect of flying my family across the Greenland icecap with a possibly unreliable engine. However, I figured that if I could maintain communication with the ground, we would have a chance of being rescued in case we were forced down onto the flat, featureless snow in Greenland's interior.

We climbed out of the deep fjord to 13,000 feet, but surprisingly found the approaching surface of the icecap rising to more than 9,000 feet above sea level. At times, we flew a mere 2,000 feet above it for stretches of hundreds of miles. The right engine was running smoothly. (The problem at Søndrestrøm never recurred and its cause was never determined. I can only speculate that it had been a temporary ice buildup at the fuel filter.) I established radio contact with a U.S. radar base called Sea Bass, where the operator said it was 22 degrees below zero and that he had me on radar 28 miles north of course.

As I turned south to get back on course, I mulled over the difficulties of navigation in this remote part of the world. VOR [very high frequency omnidirectional radio range] beacons are virtually non-existent. The INS [inertial navigation systems] used by trans-Atlantic airliners are too bulky, heavy, and expensive to fit in the 310. Even the lighter, cheaper loran [long range navigation] systems don't work reliably in these parts. There had to be a better way.

When we reached the iceberg-dotted coast it was after midnight with a beautiful Arctic sunset reflecting off our wings and tip tanks. This was truly the Land of the Midnight Sun. We'd been going since 6 A.M. and we still had 400 miles of ocean to cross in the lingering twilight. We'd had no radio communication for two hours, so I was relieved to hear a voice calling in the blind, "N76TT, this is Reykjavik. Do you read?" It was nearly dark when we landed shortly after 2 A.M.

The customs office was closed, so we trudged wearily the 100 feet to the Lofleidir Hotel, a popular spot for trans-Atlantic pilots. From the hotel room window, I could look down at our trusty 310. She looked proud to have made it. And I felt proud of my family for enduring a 20-hour day mostly cooped up in a small, noisy cabin. We were in Europe.

The next morning we left behind the glaciers and geysers of Iceland and headed for Bergen, Norway. About 70 miles out from Reykjavik, we flew low over the Vestmann Islands, where a huge volcanic eruption occurred in 1973. Nearby we saw the brand new volcanic island, Surtsey, which unexpectedly erupted from the sea in 1969. (Scientists are currently studying the place to learn how life begins.) A few hours later the Faeroe Islands appeared on the horizon, and finally the fjords of Norway. The spectacular approach to Bergen and our friendly reception to the continent were the icing on the cake.

During the next few days we flew on to Oslo and Copenhagen. From Denmark, we ventured across the German border and looked down on the city of Hamburg, heavily bombed during World War II by American B-17s. I envisioned the city in flames, but I could only wonder what the kids were thinking as they sat spellbound in the back of the plane. As we approached busy Frankfurt on the way to Zurich, the German air traffic controllers began vectoring us around all over the place. The weather was good, so I cancelled our IFR [instrument flight rules] flight plan and flew on VFR [visual flight rules], which allowed me to pretty much choose the route I wanted. More fun, too.

Flying low over the beautiful rolling countryside of southern Germany turned out to be more exciting than I'd bargained for. At one point, we slipped through a group of three parachutists, and a short while later had to dodge a graceful sailplane that suddenly appeared in the windshield. What a joy it was to cross the Swiss border and touch down in Zurich.

The ground controllers ordered us to park in a desolate area about a mile from the nearest building. We assumed somebody would drive out to pick us up and take us to customs, but we waited around for half an hour and nobody showed. The tower operator was no help at all.

Finally, we simply gathered up our luggage and started walking toward the nearest building. What a sight we were: Tom, loaded down with luggage, followed by me and the three kids in single file, trudging across the main runway at Zurich International Airport. We could easily have been mistaken for a refugee family fleeing the Iron Curtain.

Eventually we made it through customs, and then took a taxi to the Hotel Central, where we met our friends Barbara Ladyga and Tim Bentley, who drove down to meet us from their home in Göttingen, Germany. Way back in September 1986, while we were planning the trip, we promised to meet them at the Hotel Central at 4:30 on the afternoon of August 15, 1987. Isn't it remarkable, I thought, 11 months later at the exact designated time and place, here we are sitting around the table together. To celebrate our Atlantic crossing, we had a party extraordinaire, and the tension of the previous weeks finally began to melt away.

After four hours of departure preparations—most of which were spent trying to figure out an automated flight-plan filing machine that inexplicably had no instructions—we took off for Florence, Italy. N76TT was heavy that day; even though the flight to Florence wasn't very far, I had decided to fill the tanks with fuel, just to be on the safe side in strange territory. As the old saying goes, "The only time you have too much fuel is when you're on fire." So in addition to the usual load—five people, survival gear, and a whole family's luggage filled with clothes for five weeks of both cold and hot weather—we also carried a half-ton of fuel. Wouldn't you know it, the air traffic controller ordered us to climb immediately to 16,000 feet for the crossing of the Alps—3,000 feet higher than we'd been so far on the trip. I knew it would be a challenge for our non-turbocharged 310 to climb that high with such a load. Without a turbocharger, a plane gradually loses power as the air gets thinner during the climb, and at 16,000 feet, our engines would have barely half their sea level power.

Because the Alps were so close, we had to circle over the city while we climbed. Round and round we went as the altimeter slowly wound up to 8,000...10,000....12,000..... 14,000 feet. It took nearly 10 minutes to climb the last 2,000 feet. Finally at 16,000 feet, we headed south over the Alps. We were blessed with clear skies; the view of the snow-capped mountains and Lake Como below was dazzling.

On the other side of the mountains, however, a thick layer of clouds greeted us. The Italian controllers were friendly and very casual. As we neared Florence, we were directed over the airport at 7,000 feet and told, "N76TT, cleared for the approach, cleared to land." I was astonished to get the landing clearance so early. The weather was very poor, and we would have to do the complete instrument approach procedure, which from that altitude would take at least 15 minutes. Wasn't the busy city of Florence expecting any arrivals during the next quarter hour?

We followed the teardrop localizer approach procedure to the letter, descending through thick clouds and drizzle. As we got closer to the runway, we were still in the soup. If we couldn't see the runway by the time we got down to 400 feet above ground level—the MDA [minimum descent altitude]— we would have to go around and try the whole procedure again, or go to an alternate airport. Just as we reached the MDA, however, I caught a glimpse of the ground and, dead ahead, what looked like a short, narrow stretch of road.

It was the runway, barely 3,000 feet long! It turned out this was Florence's small airport for private and business planes. The big international airport, where the jetliners land, was in Pisa, home of the famed leaning tower, some 40 miles away.

The pleasant Italian customs and immigration authorities had us on our way to our final destination, Pescara, in a couple of hours. For this entire 200-mile flight we cruised just 500 feet above the countryside, seeing everything from ancient walled villages to posh, ultra-modern mountain retreats. Such contrast! Over the Adriatic Sea, I tuned in the tower at Pescara, and heard the the controller speaking Italian. Hesitantly, I spoke into the mike, "Pescara Tower, November-Seven-Six-Tango-Tango." Since English is the universal language of aviation and can be spoken in some form or another in every control tower in the world, I hoped I would be able to understand any instructions. The controller answered quickly in English (Italian accented, of course), cleared us to land and welcomed us to Pescara in an excited voice.

It turned out Fran's sister Mary Catherine and her husband Piero had told the controller of our imminent arrival. It was quite unusual for a small American plane to land there, and airport security even stationed a 24-hour armed guard at N76TT's parking spot during our stay. (You never know about those Libyan terrorists.)

After a week of fun hanging out with Mary Catherine, her husband and children, and their many friends, I was overwhelmed with the desire to keep right on flying east to Miami, the long way around. It was very frustrating to reverse course and head back home. But it had been a marvelous experience—what an education for our kids to see Europe from the window of our own airplane—and with no possibility of lost luggage!

Our flight back home took us nonstop from Pescara to the island of Jersey, England, and on to Stornaway, Scotland. There occurred the only unpleasant bureaucratic event of the trip, an outrageous $350 fee for filing a flight plan after the tower-closing time of 5 P.M. (We had arrived at 4:25, but officials conveniently delayed us until 5:05.) From Scotland, the flight back through Iceland, Greenland, and Goose Bay was uneventful—except for the moment when young Tom, swinging his opened Swiss Army knife around on a string, accidentally let it fly and skewered Michael in the forehead. Blood squirted everywhere and since we were still hours from an airport and hospital, Fran and I practically had heart attacks. The bleeding finally stopped, thank God, and no permanent damage was done.

By the time we arrived back in Miami after five weeks, Fran and I knew that someday we would make a trip that didn't require us to turn around and come back. "There's only one way to do that," I said.

2

"There were days I just wanted to call my travel agent and buy an airline ticket.**"**

I began planning our trip around the world in 1988, aiming for a departure date of June 1990. I sketched out a trial itinerary that ended up requiring an astonishing two months away from Miami. I have a rather demanding real estate business, and my immediate question was, how much is this trip really going to cost me, not only in cash but also in time absent from the business. In time, I resigned myself to the fact that if I really wanted this badly enough I would have to bite the bullet.

I wondered if the two-year preparation time would be sufficient, and marveled at the fact that Charles Lindbergh had needed just three months to raise the money, have an airplane designed and built, modify an engine for long-distance flying, and finally plan the flight itself.

I laid out a route of 29,436 miles, well above the required minimum of 22,859 miles (the distance along the tropic of Cancer or tropic of Capricorn) to be certified by the Federation Aeronautique International [FAI] as an official around-the-world flight. (The famous round-the-world flights of Wiley Post in 1931 and Howard Hughes in 1938 would not have qualified under the present rules, since they covered only 15,474 and 14,762 miles, respectively.) Many alternate routes had to be planned as well, since geo-political conditions are constantly changing.

Remembering how I had wandered off course over Greenland, and realizing that my round-the-world route would take us over dozens of remote areas without the usual radio beacons for guidance, I knew that my big problem was going to be navigation. So I began to study intensely a new satellite-based navigation system then being set up by the DOD [Department of Defense]: the $12 billion Navstar Navigational System, also called the Global Positioning System, or GPS. The satellites, designed and built by Rockwell International, were being launched by Air Force Delta II rockets from the Kennedy Space Center. At the time I began looking into the GPS, only nine satellites had been launched.

The GPS consists of a constellation of 21 satellites, plus three spares, which hurtle through space 10,900 miles above the earth in six different orbital planes. Each solar-powered Navstar satellite circles the earth every 12 hours, transmitting radio signals that describe its position. The receiver mounted in the aircraft (or boat, tank, car, or back-pack—it doesn't matter) picks up these signals, then a built-in computer calculates the receiver's precise position, altitude, heading, and speed.

Unlike ground-based systems, GPS has no propagation error, diffraction, or ionosphere and skywave interference. The signals are updated every second, so there are no inaccuracies caused by an abrupt turn of the aircraft. Best of all, it is an all-weather system, unaffected by even torrential rains.

With a GPS receiver in my aircraft, theoretically I would at all times know my position within 25 meters, my altitude within 0.1 meter, and the Universal Time within one-billionth of a second. All the limitations of other navigation systems—loran, VLF [very low frequency]/Omega, INS,

VOR, ADF [automatic direction finder], and Transit SatNav—would be eliminated with GPS. Theoretically, there would be no more worries about weather, gaps in coverage, sunspots, solar flares, precipitation, static electricity, and signal interruptions. There would be no need to install an INS.

Most Boeing 747s and other transoceanic jumbo jets are equipped with three INSs. The redundancy is for reliability. A single system might give an incorrect reading, but with only two systems giving differing readings a pilot wouldn't know which is correct. Statistics favor two of the three giving identical readings. These units cost as much as $175,000 each versus a few thousand dollars for a GPS receiver.

But would the great promise of GPS work out in the real world? I wanted to find out. Even though GPS was then in its infancy, I decided to use it for our round-the-world voyage. I would demonstrate just how good the system was. If GPS could precisely guide us across the Pacific to Australia, across the Indian Ocean, and then on the equator from the east to west coast of Africa, and finally across the Atlantic Ocean, then it would be shown that GPS could be used by anyone, anywhere. If I couldn't be the first, or the fastest, or fly around the world nonstop without refueling like the *Voyager*, I would at least be the first to circumnavigate the globe using GPS for navigation.

At the time, there was no GPS receiver on the market designed expressly for aircraft. Although several companies were beginning to manufacture GPS receivers for boats, they did not give speed readouts higher than 99 knots (about 114 mph), and I needed a groundspeed readout to help me calculate winds. However, Trimble Navigation, Ltd., in Sunnyvale, California, was developing an aircraft GPS receiver, so I called to inquire about its status, and to feel out the company about the possibility of my using one on the round-the-world trip. I was told they had a prototype under construction, and that it might be ready in time for the trip, now about 18 months away. But no promises were made. I would have to wait and see.

I purchased a set of global navigation charts [GNC] that used Lambert Conformal Conic Projection, enabling me to plot a straight line between any two points along a great circle route. Because of the curvature of the earth, the shortest distance between two distant points is not an apparent straight line, but a course that constantly changes direction along the earth's surface.

For instance, a 747 departing Tokyo does not fly due east to Los Angeles. Such a constant-heading course, or rhumb line, would be simpler to follow, but it would use far too much time and fuel. Instead, the pilot initially starts on a northeasterly course, gradually changes so that he is heading due east somewhere near the Aleutian Islands, then turns southeasterly to Los Angeles. Although the aircraft's track across the Pacific is an arc, it equates to the definition of a straight line being the shortest distance between two points because it is done across a sphere.

A great circle route is much easier to plot with Lambert charts than with Mercator charts, the type used in a road atlas and local, short-distance flight charts.

Once I sat down to plot my route around the world, the first question presented itself: which way round, west or east? Winds determined the answer. In the U.S., the prevailing wind comes from the west. But as I studied wind patterns around the world, I saw that in the equatorial regions, the wind typically blows from the east—the trade winds that sailing ships had followed for centuries. I would follow them, too. I would head west from Miami, fighting headwinds to the West Coast. There we hoped to pick up the trade winds to Hawaii and Australia, across the Indian Ocean to Africa, then the long trans-Atlantic flight to North America and home.

Most pilots are awed by the idea of flying great distances over open ocean, and once a small aircraft leaves the coastline behind, its engines invariably go into "automatic rough"—a condition entirely in the nervous pilot's ultra-attentive ear and mind. But in many ways open-water flying is easier than flying over land. There are no obstructions or rising terrain, and no other aircraft at the altitudes I would be flying. Weather for the most part is more predictable over the ocean. The world's big weather systems—hurricanes, typhoons, pressure fronts, monsoons, doldrums, and the intertropical convergence—all are born and grow over the oceans, but they are easier to predict than land-based weather. Just to be safe, I contacted the National Hurricane Center in Coral Gables, Florida, and got a special high-frequency [HF] radio frequency on which to call for position reports on any hurricanes along my route.

Obviously, we would need lots of fuel to fly such vast distances nonstop. N76TT originally had a fuel capacity of 163 gallons, good for about six hours of flying and 1,200 miles at moderate power settings. For the round-the-world trip, we would need extra fuel tanks in the nose and rear cabin, a total of ten tanks, all with various switching mechanisms, plumbing, tubes, valves, connections, and pumps. Total fuel capacity would be 430 gallons. All that fuel would weigh much more than a ton (2,580 pounds to be precise), but about 25 gallons of that 430 could not be pumped out of the bottom of the tanks. I computed the total fuel available to be 405 gallons. My fuel consumption at the typical cruising speed of just under 200 mph would be about 25 gallons per hour, so I would have enough fuel to fly 16 hours and about 3,100 miles before the tanks ran dry.

I made other modifications to the plane as well. The right engine had 1,550 hours on it, very close to the recommended time-before-overhaul of 1,700 hours. Since the trip would use up the remaining 150 hours, I'd be faced with replacing the engine right after I got back. So why not do it before I left and have the new engine for the trip? My dedicated engine mechanic, Gus Gonzales, installed a factory-remanufactured engine. He also installed a new wet compass, battery, tires, spark plugs, starters, and overhauled magnetos and alternators. An annual inspection and chemical analysis of the engine oil were performed. The logbooks and airworthiness certificates were checked and brought up to date.

Tom devoted so much time getting ready for the trip. At virtually every dinner that last year, he'd be talking about "engines this" and "GPS that." The kids started to get pretty bored with the whole subject. Their attitude was, "Get this trip over with so we don't have to hear about it any more," for which I could hardly blame them. He was almost getting to be a pain about it.

International red tape was one of the major hurdles of the trip. We have things easy here in the States; a U.S.-registered aircraft flying into the country must give only an hour's advance notice to customs. Some of the countries we'd be passing through required up to six months prior notification just to be able to fly over them. We needed innumerable letters of permission with overflight and landing permit numbers. Often we had to specify the precise day and time of arrival, as well as the precise time and place we would enter that country's airspace. To get across Africa, for example, we had to battle through the regimented rules and disorganized bureaucracies of six countries—for just one flight. I came to regret that the concept of the international border had ever been invented.

Here's a typical procedure for getting a landing or overflight permit: At least six months in advance, send a certified or registered letter to the Aviation Minister with a $1.00 prepaid postage stamp for the reply. If that fails, send a telex, along with a prepaid reply called an answer-back. If that doesn't work, save copies of your letters and telexes so that, when you show up unannounced, you can prove to foreign officials that at least you tried. (Not advisable!) Some countries also require hard copies of permits upon landing.

If all that fails, call an outfit in Houston named Base Ops, which can do the last-minute paperwork (for a stiff fee) and send it to you along the way. Fran put in many hours at the computer, and we ended up doing most of the paperwork ourselves.

I continually interviewed other pilots and friends to obtain the latest restrictions and regulations of the many countries in our flight path. I studied each country's national rules and practices pertaining to air traffic control. I checked that I had all the required entry documents to present upon arrival. Multiple copies would be needed of the certificate of ownership, general declarations, passenger, and cargo manifests, proper licenses, my pilot qualifications and certificates, aircraft log books, aircraft radio license, visas, passports, etc., etc., etc.....

No traveler's checks or credit cards would be accepted for fuel or fees. Only cash. $US was king. Some countries observe the Thursday and Friday Moslem weekend, so I tried to arrive and depart on other days so as not to be hit by exorbitant overtime charges. Any infraction of rules meant my plane could be impounded. The most serious penalty would be jail time for Fran and me. Overflight and landing permits took on a special meaning.

We became regular visitors to Dr. Caroline Macleod's Tropical Medicine and Traveler's Clinic. We got armfuls of shots: polio, tetanus, yellow fever, hepatitis, and cholera. There were also malaria pills to be taken for seven days before entering an infected area, every day while there, and for 28 days after leaving. We were ordered to avoid tap water, unless boiled, in many countries, along with uncooked foods. Tsetse flies! Dengue fever! Mosquitoes! It was all pretty scary.

Then there was all our emergency equipment. We bought a specially-designed emergency life raft with numerous life-prolonging features, including a water desalinization system. The aircraft had an ELT [emergency locater transmitter] mounted permanently in the tail that would turn on automatically in case of a sudden impact, broadcasting a signal on the 121.5mHz international emergency frequency. Fran and I would also each carry a portable ELT strapped to our legs in case we had to abandon the downed plane.

In addition, we carried an experimental EPIRB [emergency position-indicating radio beacon], which activates automatically when in contact with saltwater and broadcasts a signal to Russian and American satellites orbiting overhead. The satellites then notify ground stations in the U.S.S.R., U.S.A., Canada, and France of the downed aircraft's exact position. We finally got the experimental EPIRB from the National Oceanic and Atmospheric Administration [NOAA] after six months of begging. Interestingly, it was the exact unit that had been aboard *Voyager,* the famous long-winged craft that Dick Rutan and Jeana Yeager flew around the world nonstop in 1986.

All during the feverish preparations during late 1989 and early 1990, I kept calling the Trimble factory every two or three weeks to check on the progress of their GPS receiver prototype. Three months before the scheduled departure date, they reported that they were testing it, but still could make no promises about its availability. By this time, having made no contingency plans for another kind of long-range navigation system, I was committed to GPS. It was either going to be a Trimble or a boat receiver, and I sure didn't want to fly around the world with the groundspeed readout limited to 99 knots.

Two months before the launch date, I began to get cold feet. Maybe it was just too crazy to spend so much time, money, and effort to overcome so many obstacles and so much bureaucratic red tape. There were days I just wanted to call my travel agent and buy an airline ticket.

Despite my impatience and frustration, I was determined not to cut any corners. Every piece of equipment, every calculation, every bureaucratic procedure would be checked and rechecked. I knew I had an immense responsibility—my own survival, and that of my wife—and I realized that one moment of forgetfulness or carelessness could be the end of us. One wrong calculation could wreck the whole enterprise. My ironclad rule for the trip was simply this: No haphazard decisions!

I wanted, above all, to have a clear conscience on the day that I finally pushed the throttles forward for takeoff into the unknown. I wanted to know in my heart that I'd done everything humanly possible to make the trip safe and successful. But I also realized that I was just a fallible man, like all other men, and that despite all my best efforts, I had to accept the possibility of failure and even death. I would be ready to make peace with my Maker.

Even with all the hassles and the dangers, I really wanted to be a part of the trip. When you look back on your marriage, the things you remember are those experiences and intimacies that no one else can share. Good or bad, the flight was going to be a very intimate shared experience. I knew that when I got in that plane, there was a chance maybe I'd never see my kids again. But I wasn't going to let that stop me. I had a lot of confidence in Tom. He's the best pilot around, and he studied and prepared thoroughly.

As the time drew nearer, only a few items remained on the pretrip checklist. Trimble was taking me right down to the wire. I had enlisted the aid of Jim Cook of Palm Beach Avionics in Boca Raton, who knew people at the Trimble factory. He also started calling the factory, trying to get a commitment out of them. A week before launch, we still had no firm commitment for a GPS receiver, although Trimble had shipped Jim an installation kit and an antenna.

I decided to fly N76TT to Boca Raton so that Jim could at least install the antenna and installation kit. It was a routine flight until I pushed the gear-down lever in preparation for landing at Boca Raton. Instead of the usual "three green"—one green light for each of the two main landing gear and the nosegear that indicate they are safely down and locked—I saw the bright red gear in transit light staring me in the face and the left gear light indicating unsafe. This was trouble. The left main landing gear was not down and locked, and might collapse on landing.

I diverted to nearby Pompano Beach airport, which had a control tower. I made a low pass down the runway, and the tower said the gear appeared to be hanging down. But was it locked? One way to get a balky gear down and locked is to fly along the runway wing-down and bounce the plane on the one good main wheel, hoping the jolt knocks the loose gear into place. I tried it four times, and still the red light glowed. Back in the air again, I tried retracting the gear and cranking it down by hand, the usual "last resort" for landing gear problems. Once again, the red light blinked on.

I now had only one alternative: make a landing with a slight left yaw at touchdown, and hope that the sudden side load on the gear would knock it into the down-and-locked position. If it didn't, N76TT would flop onto its left wing tip and slide down the runway in a shower of sparks, putting my round-the-world plans on hold for a while. I brought the plane in gently and eased it onto the runway with the nose skewed to the left. Bang! The gear snapped into place, the gear light flashed green, and the plane rolled out normally.

I flew all the way to Boca Raton with the gear down and locked. There Jim Cook put the GPS installation kit and antenna in place, and Tom Pentecost spent eight hours adjusting the landing-gear rigging. Then I discovered that the radar stabilizer had failed. Although it was not a critical item, I began to wonder if the gods and gremlins were against me.

June 6, 1990. Less than a week to go now. I flew N76TT to Lakeland, Florida, to have the long-range ferry tanks and HF radio installed by Globe Aero, an aircraft-ferrying firm with extensive experience in long-distance over-water flying.

Only fully-qualified experts are legally authorized to

install the tanks. Extra fuel, of course, adds weight, about six pounds per gallon. To accommodate additional fuel tanks, the FAA may issue a temporary permit allowing a plane to takeoff at 10%, 20%, or 25% over its maximum allowable certified gross weight. It is difficult to obtain a 10% permit, more difficult to obtain a 20% permit, but most difficult to obtain the 25% over-gross-weight permit we needed. To the FAA, a pilot's credentials are a key factor for issuing a permit for the 25% overload.

When N76TT was manufactured in June 1976, it was certified for airworthiness at a gross weight of 5,500 pounds. For this trip, the FAA issued a 25% over-gross-weight permit that would allow N76TT to legally take off with a gross weight of 6,875 pounds including fuel, occupants, equipment, luggage, and everything else taken aboard.

The extra fuel tanks, which looked so small outside of the plane, filled the rear cabin to the max. The complex tanking system included three cabin tanks and one nose tank. Fuel would flow by gravity along clear plastic lines, through on-off valves, then out through the cabin floor, where it would be picked up by the engine-driven fuel pumps and distributed to the engines. But due to the design of the fuel injection system, the engines can't use all the fuel they receive, so the excess is pumped back into the plane's main wing-tip tanks, which hold 100 gallons. This system requires complex fuel management, because one must burn down the tip tanks first, to allow room for the excess fuel from the other tanks to be pumped back in. Then you have to switch back to the tip tanks to use the excess.

If one of the engine-driven fuel pumps fails, fuel from the cabin tanks, nose tank, and the plane's standard auxiliary wing tank cannot reach the engine. The only fuel available would be whatever is left in the tip tank, which is equipped with an electric standby fuel pump. If an engine-driven pump failed, I'd have, at best, four hours running time on that engine, which wouldn't do me much good in the middle of the Pacific Ocean.

The HF radio, by bouncing signals off the ionosphere, can transmit and receive for thousands of miles, far beyond the range of a normal aircraft radio. Globe Aero installed a portable ICOM 725 (a ham, or amateur, radio HF transceiver) between the seats. With it, we could talk to distant ground stations, weather forecasters, and other aircraft, as well as call for help on 8364mHz and 2182mHz, the international HF emergency frequencies.

Globe Aero strongly warned me not to fly the plane back to Miami with the long-range tanks and HF system. For one thing, the FAA permit to make these temporary modifications required that I fly via the shortest and most direct route from Lakeland to Oakland, California, my first scheduled stop on the round-the-world trip. Obviously, Miami was not along that route. But the main problem, they told me, was that eagle-eyed agents of the DEA [Drug Enforcement Administration] might spot the plane at Miami, assume that it had been equipped for drug-running, and confiscate it for months of investigation. They assured me that just such horror stories had happened many times to new aircraft legitimately tanked for overseas delivery. I still didn't have the GPS receiver installed yet, and other last-minute checks were needed. I had no choice but to head home to Miami and hope for the best.

Since fuel was expensive at Lakeland, I told the refueler to put just five gallons of fuel in each of the four ferry tanks. I figured this would be sufficient to test each tank on the flight back, which would be one of the last shakedown flights before the round-the-world departure.

After takeoff, I turned on the HF radio and called Globe Aero to check the reception. To my dismay, I could barely read them! Reception was terrible. Next I switched the fuel valve over to the newly-installed nose tank. Ten seconds later both engines quit dead. In the ensuing silence, I quickly switched back to the main tanks, and the engines caught and ran smoothly. Then I tried the forward cabin tank. Again the engines quit. Back to the mains, and they caught again. Fuming with frustration, I tried the mid and aft cabin tanks, with the same result. There I was, just days from launch, and the HF and all four ferry tanks didn't work at all. Months of reviewing various designs and configurations had gone down the drain.

The final note of this dismal flight came when I stopped off at Boca Raton to check on the status of the GPS receiver. I was told it still hadn't arrived, and there was still no guarantee from Trimble that I would get one at all.

Back in Miami, I decided I would just live with the poor HF reception, but the fuel system problem would obviously have to be solved. I filled the forward cabin tank to the top, then started the engines and switched to that tank. This time, the engines ran perfectly and kept running. Suddenly it dawned on me what the problem was: the fuel lines were connected to the tanks several inches above the bottom, to allow any water, dirt, or sediment to settle to the bottom of the tank without being sucked up by the engines—a necessary precaution since these temporary tanks did not have sumps or drains. The five gallons I'd put into each tank wasn't enough to bring the fuel level up to the fuel line pickup. The last five gallons or so in each tank were unusable. The final good news of the day came from Gus Gonzales who did a cylinder compression check on the engines: "They're perfect. All twelve cylinders are showing 75 pounds or better."

While Tom was worrying about the GPS right up until the last minute, I was making arrangements to get away from work for two months, not an easy thing to do. More importantly, I was worrying about the kids. Baby-sitters we'd arranged kept falling through, and right up until the end there was real doubt that I'd be able to go along. But a former nursery school teacher of Michael's agreed to stay at the house for the first two weeks, and his violin teacher volunteered to move in for the last eight weeks.

I also felt good that all of them would be occupied for part of the summer at a local day-camp program—Tiffany and Tom as counselors, and Michael as a camper. (Tom was also signed up for a summer school course.) Tiffany had just turned 16 and gotten her driver's license, so she would have to take a lot of responsibility. We knew she could handle it.

On Friday, June 8—the last working day before our scheduled departure on Monday—my prayers were answered: two Trimble GPS units arrived at Palm Beach Avionics! Jim Cook donated his time and expertise and installed the Trimble TNL-2000 panel-mounted receiver and a portable standby unit. The job took less than a day, and by the time Jim was finished on Friday afternoon, we had the first GPS receiver ever permanently installed in a general-aviation aircraft.

Eager to try out the GPS, and also needing to test the new compass that had just been installed, I made a quick test flight. Taking off from Boca Raton, I headed west out over the Everglades. I made several turns to the south and east, and the compass and GPS heading readouts were right on the money. Then I turned north and flew over Pahokee. Wow! A perfect position readout!

My euphoria was short-lived, however. Suddenly, the right engine began sputtering and backfiring. I switched from the nose tank to the mains, and turned on the boost pump to LOW to purge any air in the fuel lines. But it didn't help. My brand-new right engine was barely running, and sounded like it could stop dead at any moment.

I wasn't too concerned about my immediate safety, since the plane was light on fuel and could maintain altitude on one engine. But once again, I wondered if the round-the-world trip was going to be delayed. Limping back to Miami, I decided to try the HIGH setting on the boost pump. The back-firing subsided a bit, but the engine was still running rough as I came in for a landing. Terry Schuler, working late in the maintenance hangar as usual, came out to take a look. He scanned the instrument readings I'd taken. I suggested, "Maybe it's a clogged fuel nozzle. Dirt in the new tanks?"

"No, can't be," he replied.

A static run-up of the sick engine revealed that the fuel pressure was low. Without the help of the auxiliary electric fuel pump, my new factory-remanufactured engine would cough, sputter, and then stop. Terry's diagnosis: the engine-driven fuel pump had sheared and broken up internally. I was partly angry that a brand-new pump had failed, partly grateful that it hadn't broken a few days later, thousands of miles out over the ocean. The failure made me feel very vulnerable. Once again, I began to have second thoughts about this whole grand adventure. Was it such a great idea after all?

But the rush of events overcame my doubts. The

immediate problem was the time: it was after-hours on Friday evening, and we wouldn't even be able to call the factory to order a replacement fuel pump until Monday morning, the scheduled departure day. It was clear we would have to put off the flight at least a day. Resigned to the delay, Fran and I spent Saturday getting last-minute shots, and Sunday pacing in frustration over the fuel pump.

My friend Bill Kelly, a former Navy test pilot, advised us to fly the first leg of the trip nonstop to Oakland, rather then spend a night in Santa Fe, New Mexico, as we had considered doing. There were some good arguments for making a 15-hour flight right off the bat. First of all, it would be a good "dry run" of the airplane's (and our) ability to make long over-water legs, but with land always below us in case something went wrong. Second, we would make up the one-day departure delay due to the fuel pump. Finally, it would give me 15 hours to figure out how to use the GPS before it really counted.

Monday morning we decided not to wait around for a new fuel pump to be shipped from the factory, but to modify and install a similar pump that a local shop had in stock. We got telephone approval from Teledyne Continental to modify the flange of the IO-520-M pump so that it would fit my IO-520-MB. The alteration was completed Monday afternoon.

Suddenly there were no more preparations left. N76TT was ready to go. So were we.

3

"The Captain Cook Hotel was about seven miles down the road, just past a village called Banana."

It was still dark when we awoke at 4:30 A.M. on June 12, 1990. I had slept only a few hours, my head spinning from excitement and the myriad details of preparing for the round-the-world journey. Tiffany drove us to the airport, arriving at 6:30 just as the sun was coming up. As we walked out to N76TT, the sun glinted off her tip tanks. Although tail-heavy, she looked ready to go.

Leg 1: Miami to Oakland

The engines started quickly. They seemed as eager to get going as we were. We taxied slowly out for takeoff in the early morning mist, straining under the weight of 430 gallons of highly volatile aviation gasoline, grossing out at over 6,800 pounds. However, if for any reason we had to return immediately to the runway at Miami International Airport, the landing gear was certified for a stressed maximum landing weight of only 5,400 pounds.

Everything I had planned and dreamed for three years was about to begin. Would the plane even get off the ground? We were more than half a ton heavier than I'd ever taken off before, and I didn't know what to expect. When a plane is seriously overweight, the takeoff roll is much longer and it barely staggers into the air. If an engine fails, it will sink rapidly. There was no one to teach me how to fly an overweight 310—but my first lesson was about to begin.

I slowly picked up the mike. "Miami Tower, N76TT ready for takeoff, heavy, first leg around the world."

The tower replied, "Sounds wonderful, have a great trip. Cleared for takeoff." As we turned onto Runway 27 Right, the wind was 270 degrees at six knots, right on our nose. It was a good omen.

I advanced the throttles. The aircraft accelerated slowly, and, after what seemed an eternity, the airspeed indicator had inched up to 106 knots, the takeoff speed I'd calculated for our heavier weight. I gingerly pulled back on the wheel to raise the nose. At 6:53 A.M., after a 6,100-foot takeoff roll—more than three times the normal run—we were airborne.

I had filed a flight plan that would take us northwest to Sarasota, then straight across the Gulf of Mexico to New Orleans on airway GR-26. But near the LaBelle VOR, Miami Center rerouted us north to Tallahassee and then across Georgia, Alabama, and Louisiana to New Orleans—the long way around. It would cost us time and precious fuel.

Near Lakeland, I flipped on the autopilot. It would not engage! I couldn't believe it. I was going to have to hand-fly the plane for the next 15 hours. Near New Orleans, I asked for clearance to El Paso, Texas, a thousand miles further west. The air traffic controller seemed surprised. "Do you have enough fuel?"

"Affirmative," I replied. In Miami, I had filed a flight plan only for the 4-hour, 15-minute flight to New Orleans, on the theory that the FAA, DEA, and the border patrol might get suspicious about a Cessna 310 leaving south Florida with 16 hours of fuel. Near El Paso, I got another clearance all the way to Oakland. "You're going nonstop from Miami to Oakland?" the controller asked incredulously. "How much fuel you got?"

"Sixteen hours," I replied, for the first of what would be many times over the next two months. The controller was a pilot himself, and owned a single-engine Cessna 210. We chatted a while about the attributes of various aircraft, as pilots always do, and then he signed off. "Around the world, sounds like a great trip."

Over Texas, the mid-day thermals were giving us a very rough ride. The plane swayed and bucked, side to side and up and down. Then the right engine started running rough. At one point, I thought it was going to quit. Was the brand new fuel pump acting up again? With the autopilot not working it was difficult flying in such heavy turbulence while consulting the flight manual and fiddling with throttle and mixture controls. All my fiddling was to no avail, and the engine continued to run rough, although it was still putting out power. For hours and hours, we endured noise, headwinds, and getting thrown around the cockpit.

This flight from Miami to Oakland has to be the worst. I try to get into a routine of eating, exercising, and reading, but all is lost over the desert, where it is bumpy and most uncomfortable. My back hurts. My portable john malfunctions. I am miserable. Will I be able to take two months of this?

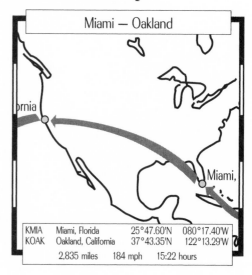

	Miami — Oakland		
KMIA	Miami, Florida	25°47.60'N	080°17.40'W
KOAK	Oakland, California	37°43.35'N	122°13.29'W
	2,835 miles	184 mph	15:22 hours

Over Arizona, I strayed off course a couple of miles. No big deal now, but later on precise navigation could be crucial. I resolved to pay better attention and concentrate on following those airways that stretched ahead to California.

Finally, the green golf courses and blue swimming pools of Palm Springs, California, came into view. But after the detour around the Gulf and the headwinds over the desert, did we have enough fuel to make Oakland? I doubted it. We'd probably have to land at Bakersfield, get a little fuel, and continue on up to Oakland. As we approached Bakersfield, I realized that Oakland was only an hour away. I estimated we had 90 minutes of fuel left. A 30-minute reserve would be cutting it a bit close, but the weather was clear, and air traffic control assured us there would be no traffic delays. The right engine was still running rough, but had not gotten any worse. I decided to go for it.

The mountains of California were incredibly beautiful as we cruised northward. Approaching the southern tip of San Francisco Bay, off to the left we could see Silicon Valley and Sunnyvale, where Trimble was located and our GPS receivers were born. As the setting sun reflected off the water, we were cleared down to 12,000 feet, then 11,000, 8,000, and 4,000. Just after we leveled off over Hayward at 2,500 feet came the words we'd been waiting 15 hours and 22 minutes to hear: "N76TT, cleared to land, Runway 27 Right." Squeak...squeak, touchdown.

We'd made it. Although navigation with the GPS had been easy, headwinds, rain, turbulence, and two weather fronts had challenged us. All of my pilot peers had told me that flying around the world east to west was the wrong way. So far, it looked like they were correct.

The next morning, I had to solve two major problems

before we could continue on the next leg to Hawaii: the inoperative autopilot and the rough-running engine. A local mechanic quickly discovered the engine problem. After pulling the spark plugs and finding them okay, he took out the fuel injector nozzles. They were badly plugged, apparently the result of dirt in the fuel. He cleaned them out, reinstalled them, and did an engine run-up. Perfect.

The autopilot problem, unfortunately, was not solved so quickly. The first avionics shop we tried diagnosed a bad computer amplifier. They tried to fix it, but after an hour, threw up their hands. Shop number two, Bay Avionics, tried for two hours to repair it before giving up. "Can't be fixed," they said. When I asked about the possibility of replacing the amplifier with a new or rebuilt one, they said none was available anywhere in California. They'd try to locate one somewhere else tomorrow morning, Thursday.

The next day, Bay Avionics began calling all over the country, and finally got a "yes" from Airwick Aviation in Wichita, Kansas. They had a used one, and figured it might work. But they'd have to test it. They'd let us know.

With time to kill, I decided to "swing" N76TT's new compass, which means to align and calibrate it using a circular grid laid out on the tarmac. We taxied out to the old Navy compass rose, pointed the nose due north, then at each 30° increment checked the compass reading in various configurations—radios on and off, HF on and off, and then all electrical systems off, simulating a complete electrical failure. I wondered how many historic long-distance flights across the Pacific had begun at this compass rose, and how many of them had met with disaster.

I also tested the HF radio. This was a critical test. Before any aircraft is granted a clearance across the Pacific

Ocean, it must establish contact with San Francisco Radio on the proper HF frequencies. So far, I'd not managed to communicate with anyone on it, except for that first weak, scratchy conversation back in Florida. I switched to the proper channel, and finally, after a lot of static, I heard San Francisco Radio talking to a Honolulu-bound American 747 that had blown a tire on takeoff. I called repeatedly, but apparently no one could hear me. I'd just have to try again when we were ready to go for real.

More problems surfaced. I discovered that I had lost the Oakland-to-Hawaii GPS computer satellite position readouts. This was critical information. I figured I'd left them back at our hotel restaurant, and Fran and I spent a frantic hour searching, even going through the hotel garbage. No luck.

But we had to keep going with our preparations, and I taxied over to the fuel pumps to fill up the nearly empty tanks. The nose tank took 19.6 gallons, 43.9 in the right tip, 25.6 right auxiliary, 30.0 left auxiliary, 44.7 left tip, 69.5 front cabin tank, 68.2 mid, 70.9 aft. The total came to 372.4 gallons. Add the 12 useable gallons remaining when we landed at Oakland, and the total usable fuel came to 384.4 gallons. Something was wrong. I was supposed to have 400 gallons of usable fuel. The missing 15.6 gallons cut more than half an hour of flight time and 100 miles off our maximum range. This was not a good situation! I would be uncertain about our exact fuel supply when flying over the Pacific Ocean. Perhaps the tanks were tilted slightly and couldn't hold their full capacity. One more uncertainty.

Finally, at sunset, a bit of good news. We got word from Kansas that, yes, the autopilot computer amplifier worked, and would arrive in Oakland Friday morning by 9:30. Just one problem: Bay Avionics was going to be closed on Friday. The owners were taking the day off to go fishing, so they couldn't install the new part. I had but one choice: install it myself.

We were up at 6:30 the next morning, had a quick breakfast and blasted off to the Federal Express office, arriving exactly as they opened at 8:00 A.M. The computer amplifier had arrived! We had a frustrating half-hour wait for a taxi to take us back to the airport, where I immediately went to the FAA Flight Service Station [FSS] to file the flight plan. To my surprise, they would not accept the great-circle route that I had so carefully plotted, but required that I fly the standard route, airway Romeo 464, which is significantly longer. To file the new flight plan, I had to figure out in my head all the estimated flight times between the new checkpoints.

It was 9:30 before we finally got to the airplane, where I began to install the new autopilot part. It didn't take long, and I was rather pleased with myself as I turned on the autopilot for a routine ground check. !@#$%&*. It didn't work.

With Bay Avionics "gone fishin'," I had no choice but to appeal to the space cadets who'd first tried to work on the autopilot. I cancelled the flight plan, then flagged down a fueling truck to take us to a telephone to call them. As luck would have it, we passed a third avionics shop on the way to the telephone. The truck screeched to a halt, and we piled out and knocked on the door of Tower Avionics. A fellow named Ron Hitchcock listened to my desperate story. Well, he said, he happened to be the best Cessna 400B autopilot fixer in the nation, but no, he just didn't have time to fix mine today. He had three technicians out sick or on vacation, and since he was the foreman, he didn't do the sort of routine bench work that we needed.

Desperate, I summoned up all the persuasive techniques I'd ever learned. I begged. I pleaded. I cajoled. I flattered him shamelessly with fawning compliments. It worked. He agreed to take a look, but for no more than 15 minutes. Great! He pulled the computer amplifier, put it on the test bench, and declared it adequate, but nothing spectacular. (Apparently, it had only 14 of 19 required modifications.) He also tested my original amplifier, and though it had only 3 of the 19 mods, it too was adequate and should not have caused the failure to engage that we'd experienced.

After we took Ron to his favorite restaurant for lunch, one of his technicians began tinkering with the autopilot, and discovered a burned-out relay in the wing. "How long to fix it?" I asked.

"Well, we'd have to order a new part. It's already 3:30 back east where the factory is; too late for them to ship today. They could ship it Monday, we'd get it Tuesday, I'd install it, and you could be on your way Wednesday."

My heart sank. We'd already waited three days in Oakland; next Wednesday would put us eight days behind schedule before we even got off the mainland. At this point I felt like tucking my tail between my legs, heading back to Miami and just forgetting this whole ridiculous idea. But Fran wouldn't let me. She insisted I keep trying.

Are we nuts? I'm not used to sitting around airports and repair shops, drinking coffee and reading old newspapers. I'm a professional dietitian, a busy mom, and a community volunteer always with something on my schedule. This waiting is tortuous. I do my exercises and focus on positive thinking. A good book in my bag is a necessary part of any preflight planning. Food helps, too. We have Mexican with the guys from the second repair shop and

Chinese with the people from the third. Everybody is so nice and understanding of our predicament. It's quite chilly in Oakland, especially in the morning. I hear a slight hoarseness in Tom's voice. Perhaps the flu?

I asked if there was any possible way to find a relay—new, rebuilt, used, any relay that worked—somewhere on the airport. Ron said he'd see what he could do. After a couple of hours, he announced that a relay had been found. He installed it. It worked.

I was almost too numb to be elated. This trip was supposed to be fun, but I kept wondering when the fun was going to start. That night back in the hotel I was sick, shivering with a cold, coughing, sore throat, and serious laryngitis. But we were up before six, had a quick breakfast and headed for the FSS to file the new flight plan. The government guys wanted to talk, not file, but I finally got out of there and to the plane, where Fran was waiting with the luggage. It was lonely out on the ramp; a cold, windy, rainy, foggy morning, somewhat reminiscent of the airport scene in the movie *Casablanca*. We climbed aboard with no fanfare.

Leg 2: Oakland to Kona

Both engines were eager to go, and they sounded particularly strong. I turned the audio panel switch on and felt a surge of excitement. I asked for my IFR clearance to Kona, Hawaii. We were cleared as filed. Then Oakland ground control came back with "N76TT, taxi Runway 29." With the heavy load of fuel, we had to taxi at a snail's pace, and it took us 22 minutes from engine start to the point where we turned carefully onto the long, 10,000-foot runway and put the nose wheel on the centerline.

When the takeoff clearance came, I smiled for the first time in days. It was so exciting to push the throttles forward as far as they'd go and feel the acceleration as the Cessna aimed for the opposite end of the runway. I had already checked the compass, the directional gyro [DG], and all the engine instruments, so all I had to do was keep the nose straight and watch as the airspeed needle slowly climbed toward the takeoff speed of 106 knots. We rolled on and on, and I remembered not to force the lift-off. Finally, when the needle hit 106, I pulled gently back on the wheel and we lifted off into the fog and drizzle. "N76TT, turn left 220 degrees direct Bebop, contact San Francisco Control on 131.95 for HF frequency assignment." Fran looked over at me and smiled.

I am filled with emotions—confident yet fearful. Anticipating and praying. Suddenly, we break out on top of the clouds into a bright blue sky! I see some mountain tops to the north and the towers of the Golden Gate Bridge poking out of the clouds. It's so exciting. I'm crying.

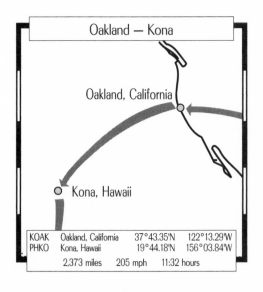

Oakland — Kona			
KOAK	Oakland, California	37°43.35'N	122°13.29'W
PHKO	Kona, Hawaii	19°44.18'N	156°03.84'W
	2,373 miles	205 mph	11:32 hours

I banked the plane toward Bebop navigational fix, called San Francisco Control on the standard aircraft VHF radio, and got my primary and secondary HF frequencies. As I switched from VHF over to the HF radio, I was very concerned. The HF set had to work this time, or I would be forced to turn back. I tried five transmissions, on both assigned HF frequencies with no response. My last call to San Francisco on VHF had been very weak by the time I had gotten to Bebop, and the controller had told me to stay on the HF from then on. I tried again on the assigned HF frequency. Nothing. The HF radio simply wasn't working. I decided to keep going and improvise.

To complicate matters, the GPS wasn't working either. Only two satellites were above the horizon at that moment, not enough for the GPS receivers to compute an accurate position. Not only was I incommunicado with ground controllers, I also didn't know exactly where I was. If only there were more than 11 GPS satellites in orbit, I thought. Then I wouldn't have such gaps in coverage. Maybe I shouldn't be using GPS as a primary navigation system. I held my dead reckoning heading to Bluff, the next position fix and mandatory reporting point.

At the time I calculated we should be at Bluff, I switched to the emergency VHF frequency of 121.5mHz and was able to contact an American Airlines 747 high overhead, also on the way to Hawaii. After we both switched to 123.45mHz, I asked him to relay my position report to San Francisco Control. Thank God, he had no return message with orders to turn back. The American captain signed off with, "It's a mighty little island to find in a mighty big ocean. Good luck, Cessna." Considering that at that moment I had no working navigational devices whatsoever, I figured I'd take all the luck I could get.

Fortune smiled shortly thereafter; both GPS units came to life and their displays agreed with each other. At last, I knew our precise location—and it wasn't too far off what I'd estimated with dead reckoning. Better yet, the GPS groundspeed readout indicated that we were beginning to pick up a nice tailwind, just as I had hoped.

The HF radio also began to awaken, and I could occasionally hear other aircraft. When we got to Bakon fix, the next reporting point, I tried calling San Francisco once more. "Cessna November-Seven-Six-Tango-Tango, Bakon nineteen-twenty-five Zulu, flight level zero-eight-zero, ETA Billo twenty-one-fifteen Zulu. Beats next."

Translated, that means I was at the Bakon reporting point at 7:25 P.M. (1925Z) Greenwich time, flying at 8,000 feet, my estimated time of arrival at the next fix, Billo, was 9:15 P.M. (2115Z), and that the next reporting point after that was Beats. (These theoretical navigational points in space, called "fixes" and "intersections," are given concocted five-letter names such as Bebop, Bakon, and Billo to preclude any confusion with genuine place names.)

San Francisco answered faintly, but with bad news—they could make out only my call sign, nothing else. Then, loud and clear, Honolulu Radio broke into the frequency. Aloha! The beautiful voice of a Hawaiian lady more than 2,000 miles away said she'd heard me loud and clear, and would relay my position report to San Francisco.

I knew high-frequency radio transmissions could be quirky, but it seemed odd that I was picking up a station 2,000 miles away better than one 200 miles away. Thinking it over, I surmised that perhaps it was the position of the HF antenna, which stretched from the tip of the tail to the top of the cabin and then to the nose, pointed more or less toward Honolulu. Remembering that best HF reception is achieved when a long-wire antenna is at a right angle to the transmitting station, I turned 90° to the right. Fran looked at me like I was crazy.

There we were over the ocean, hundreds of miles from land, flying first due north for five minutes then due south for five minutes, attempting to improve my transmissions to San Francisco. We never did make contact.

We had picked up a nice tailwind, the GPS was working flawlessly, and it was a great feeling to be heading west toward Miami—the long way around. For once, we wouldn't have to turn around to go home! But things began to go wrong quickly. The autopilot, although it was holding heading properly, could not maintain a steady altitude. N76TT would porpoise slowly up and down several hundred feet. In exasperation, I turned off the altitude-hold function.

After about six hours, we reached Billo reporting point, roughly halfway between San Francisco and Hawaii. Being halfway, or at the equidistant point, is a significant milestone on an over-water leg of 2,064 nautical miles. Deciding which land mass to swim toward might cause a family argument if we were in the drink.

Actually, just behind us was a more significant milestone, our equitime point. Depending on the direction and velocity of the winds aloft at various altitudes, the equitime point and the equidistant point may be different. Beyond the equitime point, in case of trouble, we would simply keep going rather than turn back.

Wouldn't you know it, right about then, when we were about as far as we could possibly get from land, the right engine started to run rough. This was not a barely perceptible "automatic rough," but a severe vibration, with the engine banging and shaking. Meanwhile, the cylinder head temperature started to drop towards the bottom of the green. Fuel wasn't getting to the cylinders.

I figured that the fuel injector nozzles were getting

plugged up with junk in the fuel tanks again, so I tried richening the mixture and turning on the boost pump to increase the fuel flow to the engine. After a half-hour or so of fiddling, the engine ran smoothly again. But I was concerned; the brand new engine had yet to complete a leg of the trip without misfiring. There was nothing more to be done about it up here; I'd worry about it later. We droned on through the clear Pacific sky.

Time seems to be standing still. My feet are cold. I try to find a comfortable place for them, propped between or above the rudder pedals, with my calves resting on the life raft. The light-weight steel cabin tanks make tortuous bending noises again as the fuel runs out. They bulge when they are full, but as they empty the sides contract. I jump every time I hear the loud bang. It is even more nerve-racking when I can see air bubbles moving through the clear fuel lines near my feet. Since these temporary tanks don't have fuel quantity gauges, the air bubbles mean a tank is empty. Immediately the engines sputter and I think of the sharks below. Tom is always alert, and he quickly switches to another tank.

A while back Tom told me to smile. I get too worried about things I don't understand. I guess I have to be reminded that things are okay, to ease up, to relax a little.

We were near the "point of no return" (the place where I wouldn't have enough fuel to return to California) about 900 miles out from Honolulu with the GPS reading 27°52.66' north latitude and 148°03.43' west longitude. We started to pick up Hawaiian music over the ADF [automatic direction finder], which homes in on radio signals in the AM commercial broadcast band. It was a big psychological boost to hear our destination so clearly and see the ADF needle trying to point dead ahead. Finally, several hours later, we entered the Honolulu FIR [flight information region], at which point planes are required to make contact with Honolulu Control. We were only about 100 miles out, close enough to call them up on the good old VHF radio.

Honolulu cleared us to Cluts fix, and then to the Upp VOR over Upolu Point. We'd had near-perfect weather all the way across, but as we neared landfall the cumulonimbus clouds began to build and soon we were in rain. The controller then ordered us to hold at Vicki intersection. I couldn't believe it. After more than eleven hours of flying in clear weather, we were being held up just a few miles from our destination in the pouring rain.

Finally we were cleared for the ILS/DME [instrument landing system/distance measuring equipment] Runway 17 approach to Kona, a small airport on Hawaii's Big Island. After 11 hours, 32 minutes aloft, we touched down. It was about 5 P.M., and everyone seemed to have gone home for the day. (Thank God for statehood; we didn't have to clear customs or immigration.) A lone security guard waved us down and asked rather tersely how we had gotten past the fence and into the airport restricted area. She gaped in astonishment when we told her we'd just flown in from Oakland in that little plane over there.

When we call home, Tiffany tells us she ran the car into a guard pole at McDonald's, damaging the front bumper and hood. Fortunately, no one was hurt. What a feeling. We are so far away from our children; there is nothing we can do for them.

Leg 3: Kona to Christmas Island

On Monday, June 18, we took off for Christmas Island, a tiny dot on the chart some 1,200 miles to the south. In the same big ocean about which the 747 pilot had warned us, our destination was an even tinier island. Normally, a small plane would have to simply dead-reckon toward the island and hope not to be blown too far off course to pick up the island's radio homing beacon. With GPS, I could fly a precise course with complete confidence, and not worry about picking up the beacon.

As it turned out, the GPS made all the difference on this leg. A couple of hours into the flight, Honolulu Control called urgently and said that a passing military aircraft had just reported Christmas Island's 333mHz beacon out of service, and what were our intentions? "Can't stop now," I replied. "We're continuing on to Christmas Island." I had complete confidence in the GPS.

About 11 degrees north of the equator—roughly halfway there—we ran into the rains of an ITC [intertropical convergence]. An old aviator I'd met in Florida had told me all about this phenomenon, a zone of converging weather patterns where it rains almost constantly. But, he assured me, there was virtually never any lightning or turbulence, and therefore little danger. He was right. The rains appeared as predicted, and we cruised through with no problems.

The GPS worked perfectly. Right on schedule, we popped out of a cloud and there it was, a beautiful little island covered with palm trees, right in front of us. The GPS guided us literally to the end of the runway. Total flight time was six hours, 43 minutes.

We were met by a barefoot customs man, who told us that no visa was required, just a few forms. That came as a surprise and relief, since we'd spent several months and hundreds of dollars in phone and telex messages—and even enlisted the help of the British Embassy in Washington—in a vain attempt to get a visa. We decided to simply show up without one and take our chances. I figured the worst they could do was tell us to leave.

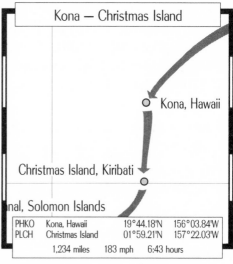

Kona — Christmas Island

Kona, Hawaii

Christmas Island, Kiribati

nal, Solomon Islands

PHKO	Kona, Hawaii	19°44.18'N	156°03.84'W
PLCH	Christmas Island	01°59.21'N	157°22.03'W
	1,234 miles	183 mph	6:43 hours

The island is covered with palms planted in rows. An old weather-beaten tower is on one side of the runway and a shack-like terminal on the other. The customs man gives us a ride on the back of an open truck that has benches along the sides and a wooden roof. A native woman rides with us part of the way. She is very open, smiling, and inquisitive.

The Captain Cook Hotel was about seven miles down the road, just past a village called Banana. We talked with four young American men from a sailboat on the way to Bora Bora. They thought flying small planes over the ocean sounded pretty dangerous, but I told them it looked to me like they were the ones in danger on such a small boat. Of course, they didn't agree.

We walk to the beach where huge waves are breaking on the coral reef. Meet three Australians who are reef fishing; one caught a large trevaria fish. Take photos.

We sit with the Aussies at dinner, along with four Japanese divers (including one woman). Everyone is curious about our trip. The Australians brought the fish they caught as a dinner treat for the Japanese, who gave them lobster the night before. The cook serves part of the fish raw, sashimi-style, which they eat with chopsticks. In addition to the fresh fish, there are hearts-of-palm salad, rice, coconut bread, broccoli, and onions seasoned with sage. Dessert is frozen cheesecake—probably Sara Lee!

The small gift shop has some woven palm baskets and table mats, fishing supplies, very old T-shirts, and—inexplicably—perhaps as many as a hundred large-sized bras hanging about.

Beautiful stars, extraordinarily bright. Southern Cross. Surf glowing, wonderful breeze. Tom's cough seems to be gone. Sleep.

Leg 4: Christmas Island to Pago Pago

The next day we were off to Pago Pago (pronounced *Pango Pango*) on American Samoa, almost 1,500 miles further south. We had no problem talking to Honolulu on the HF radio to activate our flight plan. As we approached the equator, we watched the latitude readout on the GPS receiver as it counted down. When it blinked 00°00.00', we snapped a photo, and then followed with the old nautical tradition and clinked our water jugs together in a toast to the sea god Neptune, lest he snatch us out of the sky. It was the first of four equatorial crossings on the trip.

During most of this seven-hour-plus flight, the HF radio was useless, and we lost all contact with the outside world. We entertained ourselves by reading tourist guidebooks.

The only sign of life we see, about three hours out, is a boat I spot heading due west. That's it. For one period of an hour or so, there isn't a cloud anywhere—just endless blue ocean and endless blue sky. We are the only creatures out here—at least the only human creatures. I'm starting to get used to these long flights.

About 500 miles from Pago Pago, the ADF needle came to life, swinging back and forth in an attempt to home on the feeble 403mHz signal from the NDB [non-directional beacon]. About 150 miles out, I faintly heard Pago Pago calling in the blind for N76TT. They were expecting us! Human contact at last! In a bit of poetic irony, the international phonetic pronunciation of "T" in an aircraft call sign happens to be Tango, so it was a case of Pango Pango calling Tango Tango.

"There it is!" I gasped. Lush, beautiful volcanic mountains sloped breathtakingly down to the blue Pacific. We flew down the coastline, dodging rain clouds that were beginning to build up, then flew between two tall peaks of the mountain range to the airport on the other side. I reported the airport in sight, and we were cleared for a visual approach to Runway 5. We touched down lightly, since there were only 60 gallons of fuel aboard. Taxiing to the fuel pumps, we saw a U.S. Air Force C-141 being serviced while en route from Australia to Hawaii. Our elapsed time had been seven hours, 45 minutes.

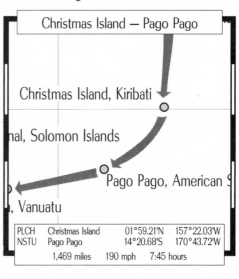

American Samoa was beautiful from the air, but we

saw paper, cans, and piles of trash scattered along the winding roads. These eyesores made us wonder if the $93 million American taxpayers spend each year to support this territory was being wasted. The countryside of Western Samoa, on the other hand, was clean and tidy everywhere we went. It receives little aid from anyone, but its people have great pride in their independent little nation.

Some of the local customs are a bit unusual. We can't get over the men wearing lavalavas, or skirts of printed cloth hanging just below the knees. The typical Samoan businessman wears a shirt, tie, dress shoes, socks, and a lavalava. Nicely tailored, of course.

One day we take a boat across to the small island of Aunuui. On board, we meet a girl named Fia and her cousin, who were taking home supplies and gas for cooking. They take us on a grand walking tour of the island—through a real tropical jungle, past a field full of huge jumping frogs, a lake of quicksand, and a Japanese fishing boat that had run aground. We stop at a house, where an old man gives us a soda. Finally, Fia convinced someone she knew with a boat to take us back to the main island. We promise to send her a photo.

When we call home and talk to Tom, he greets us with, "What do you want?" Apparently they're doing okay without us.

Leg 5: Pago Pago to Port Vila

On June 25, after taking on 327 gallons of fuel, we departed Pago Pago for Port Vila, in the Vanuatu Islands. The 1,400-mile route would take us right over Fiji. The first hour after takeoff was extremely busy—setting up GPS navigation waypoints, calculating estimates to places we had never heard of, and of course coping with the usual trouble of transmitting messages over the HF radio. We also had our first experience with a special compass we'd brought along for use in the southern hemisphere. It was modified and calibrated to account for the pull of the south magnetic pole, which has a significant influence on compass readings. This fact isn't well known, and many planes have probably been lost because of it.

As we flew, it seemed that we had arrived in paradise. Majestic, lush volcanic mountains thrust up out of the sea as we flew on through the Samoan Islands. We were looking firsthand at the geologic evolution of the islands of the South Pacific, from volcanoes erupting at the ocean floor, surging upward and emerging above the surface, to the coral reefs and sediments that accumulated over millions of years to form shelves and barrier reefs around them. The final stage of the evolution was the atoll, a ring-shaped coral island that surrounds a calm interior lagoon.

We crossed the International Date Line just west of Western Samoa. One moment it was 12 noon on June 25, 1990; the next moment it was 12 noon on June 26, 1990. Time flies when you're having fun. We were in the same general area in which Amelia Earhart had disappeared 60-odd years ago, and I was very mindful of the fragility of our little Cessna—and of the importance of precise navigation.

After about three hours, a stunningly beautiful atoll appeared below us, then another. We dropped down to 4,000 feet. We were approaching the 800 islands of Fiji, perhaps the most beautiful in all the world, but so remote that few people ever see them—especially from such a low altitude. We made radio contact on the regular VHF radio, and were instructed to climb to 12,000 feet to overfly the international airport on the big island of Viti Levu, Fiji. (We had read that we would be charged a substantial communication fee to cross Fijian airspace, but were never sent a bill.) As we crossed the rugged mountains and tropical forests of Viti Levu, we saw two small rain showers drifting over the island, throwing off spectacular rainbows.

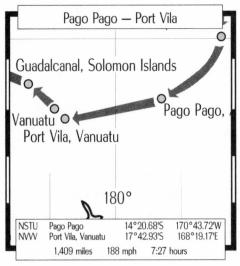

Pago Pago — Port Vila

Guadalcanal, Solomon Islands

Vanuatu
Port Vila, Vanuatu

Pago Pago,

180°

NSTU	Pago Pago	14°20.68'S	170°43.72'W
NVVV	Port Vila, Vanuatu	17°42.93'S	168°19.17'E
	1,409 miles	188 mph	7:27 hours

We flew three more hours in light-to-moderate rain before sighting Port Vila. Once again, the GPS had performed flawlessly all the way, and for the third leg in a row the right engine had given no trouble. We were cleared down to 3,200 feet, then a right-hand "circuit" to a smooth landing. Flight time was seven hours, 27 minutes.

The customs people had left minutes before our arrival. Everyone was called back, but no one seemed to worry about it; they were pleasant and relaxed. No hypertension here. I taxied the plane over to a grassy area, and a young pilot named Pierre offered his assistance for anything we might need for the plane. I asked him if security was a problem, and he assured me the plane would be fine. "Don't worry. Be happy." Then he invited Fran and me to the Aero Club for a beer. We ended up staying at a lovely hotel called Le Lagon, which offered pilots a 50-percent discount.

At the reception desk we are presented with a "welcome aboard" drink—some type of fruit juice. Should we drink it? Oh, well, take a chance! People are relaxing around the pool and taking canoes out into the lagoon. Dinner is carvery style and we go nuts over the roast lamb. It is a very clear night and the stars are unbelievable. I'm getting used to seeing the Southern Cross. We watch PT-109 *on TV. How appropriate since we will be arriving at Guadalcanal in a couple of days.*

The next day I buy a straw bag—all the women have one—and spears for the boys back home. See Bloody Mary's Bar and outdoor restaurant. Native women sit in the shade with their wares for sale—bananas, coconuts, fruit, cloth, and baskets.

Leg 6: Port Vila to Santo

Our next leg was a short 150-mile jaunt north to Santo, on Espiritu Santo, an island that served as the staging point for Allied forces in World War II during the battle for Guadalcanal. I wanted to relive a part of that history. The flight took us over several more exotic islands, and as we approached to land at Santo, I noticed flashing lights at the end of the runway. Five fire and rescue trucks were standing by; apparently they had received advance word of my landing techniques. Fortunately, their services were not required.

At Santo, we immediately filed our flight plan for the next leg to the Solomon Islands, which must be done at least 24 hours in advance of the flight. This allowed us a full day to explore Espiritu Santo. We found Edward, a taxi driver and guide, who took us around to the historic spots on the island. I remembered from my World War II studies reading about Bomber No. 3 Airfield, where B-17s were launched into combat toward the Solomons, along the same route we would soon be flying. The runway was about 7,000 feet long and built on a flat area in the high country. We found the abandoned airstrip, partly taken over by grass, but still mostly intact.

I imagined the sound of overloaded B-17s roaring

down the runway, straining to fly in the tropical heat. Fran noticed something shining out in a nearby field, and Edward got permission from the landowner for us to walk out and look at it. It turned out to be the bent and twisted wing of a B-17, apparently undisturbed by tourists or treasure hunters. Later we saw a Navy version of the old Beech 18 that had been pulled from the water, and was now sitting on a beach. Rusting Quonset huts could be found all over the island, more remnants of the war 50 years ago. Later that evening we saw a documentary film about the sinking of the SS *Calvin Coolidge* in Santo's harbor.

We walk up and down the main street looking into Japanese-operated, all-purpose stores selling everything from clothes, food, and toys to mattresses and Chinese toilet paper. The natives seem more "native" than ever. By comparison, Vila had been quite sophisticated. Women wear muumuus (ground-length Mother Hubbard shifts introduced by the missionaries to cover nakedness) with ribbons tied in a bow on the puffed sleeves. People seem thinner. Lots of pot holes on the dusty roads. Cars and trucks are being abused.

The proprietress of our hotel was a stunning woman from Malawi, in Africa, named Mary Jane Dink. She had wandered around the world for years before settling on this island, which was also the place where James Michener was stationed during his military service and where he conceived his novel *South Pacific*.

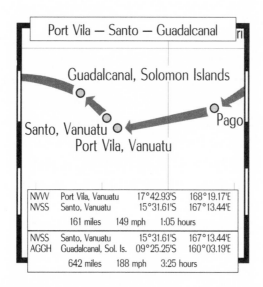

NVV	Port Vila, Vanuatu	17°42.93'S	168°19.17'E
NVSS	Santo, Vanuatu	15°31.61'S	167°13.44'E
	161 miles	149 mph	1:05 hours
NVSS	Santo, Vanuatu	15°31.61'S	167°13.44'E
AGGH	Guadalcanal, Sol. Is.	09°25.25'S	160°03.19'E
	642 miles	188 mph	3:25 hours

Leg 7: Santo to Guadalcanal

The next morning, after confirming our flight plan, we headed for the Solomon Islands. Our destination was Guadalcanal, about 600 miles away. As we cruised past Santo's mountains, dark blue waters, and virgin beaches, we found once again that the HF radio wasn't picking anything up. But we managed to make contact eventually on VHF, and three hours later the island that looms so large in naval history came into view. Before landing, we made a brief detour up "The Slot" to Savo Island, the scene of so many horrific naval battles, circled it once, and then returned to Henderson Airfield, the airstrip for which 36,000 men died. Originally only 2,200 feet long, it has since been lengthened to 5,500 feet, just barely long enough for us to take off with a heavy load of fuel.

After landing at Guadalcanal, we walked over to the Shell office on the airport. They told us the aircraft fuel storage tank was contaminated, and they couldn't sell us any. Uh-oh. If we couldn't get fuel here, we'd be facing a major problem; we did not have enough fuel on board for the next leg, the 1,900-mile flight to Darwin, Australia.

Well, they admitted, they did have a few old 55-gallon drums of avgas lying around somewhere. I said that would do fine, and it took four hours, pumping the gas out of the barrels by hand, to fuel the aircraft. I also bought six quarts of the only oil available, which came in plain cans and was of unknown origin. Then I noticed a puddle of red fluid under the right wing—the landing gear strut was leaking badly. Of course it was late Friday afternoon, and no mechanic would be available until Monday morning. Oh, well. At least we had the weekend to explore the rich military history of the island.

Once again, we found a local driver who was eager to give us a tour of the island. We visited Red Beach, where 10,000 American GIs stormed ashore; Bloody Ridge, where the battle was fought that turned the tide in the Pacific War (28,000 Japanese killed, along with 8,000 Americans); a 28-room underground communications bunker built by the Japanese but captured by the Americans and turned into a hospital. We also visited a museum in a Seventh-Day Adventist school that had on display a Bell P-39 fighter and a Douglas Dauntless dive-bomber.

Talking to a local islander, we learned that a DC-3 had been recently found crashed in the jungle, still loaded with ammunition. Land mines and unexploded shells were everywhere on the island, and we were advised to be careful where we stepped if we got off the beaten path. And there was another somewhat less dangerous legacy of the American presence: one million Coke bottles that had been discarded by GIs.

Sunday we find an Anglican church where the music is inspiring. Deacons and servers are barefoot. Later we drive up the hills above the city; the road is very rough. In spots where bridges are needed there are none—we just drive through the water. All along we see forests of palms, gorgeous views of the ocean, and many people. They seem to be walking home after a Sunday soccer game or visiting friends. They smile and wave. We stop and talk to a group of girls carrying bundles on their heads. They were picking fern cabbage that they wrap in banana leaves as a salad for dinner. They think we are Peace Corps workers because we speak English.

We ran into a New Zealander named John Murray who was a captain with Solomon Airlines, flying its one jet, a Boeing 737-300. As pilots inevitably do, we got to telling flying stories, and he described how the previous month he'd gotten lost en route to Tonga. It seems that a particularly strong solar flare had disrupted his fancy VLF/Omega navigation system, which relies on very low-frequency signals from ground stations. I told him about my GPS system, about how it was not affected by solar flares or anything else, and about how it cost perhaps one-tenth the price of his VLF/Omega system. He seemed amazed to hear that a Cessna had a better navigation system than he did, and said he would try to talk his employer into buying a GPS system.

Even though we hear it can be dangerous wandering around Guadalcanal at night, we decide to venture out for some local cuisine. We find La Perouse, a little restaurant on a beach a ways out of town. As we sit down, we overhear how the night before a large snake had fallen out of the thatched roof onto the table of some unsuspecting tourists. So when a big old lizard drops out of the ceiling onto our table a little while later, it doesn't seem so bad. We enjoy fish soup and prawns with garlic and tomatoes. Are we crazy eating prawns after all the warning from our doctor? Maybe not. The waitresses are barefoot. The elegant Gilbertese dancers wear wispy grass skirts and each has a scarlet hibiscus in her hair. This night is magical.

Tom stays up late, anticipating the flight to Darwin. He goes over and over everything, and then again.

Monday morning, we got up early to find a mechanic to fix the leaking landing gear strut. We'd been told that one might arrive at 7:30, but we didn't arrive till 7:45 due to a traffic delay. I walked toward the plane and was astonished to see it sitting level, rather than cocked over on the flat strut as we'd left it, with the wingtip almost scraping the ground. It looked fixed! It was fixed. Barry, the guy who'd sold us the oil, had already pumped it up, without even being asked. He even apologized for not having the proper parts and equipment to permanently fix the leak. And there was no charge.

It would take a new seal and some more hydraulic fluid to properly fix the strut, but I figured it would be okay at least to Darwin, where it could be repaired. Now we could get an early start for the 11-hour flight to Darwin. We were already fueled, and all we needed was a stamp on our passports and we'd be on our way.

The customs man said that the immigration people would be there shortly. "Shortly" turned into a half hour, then an hour, then two hours. I had to refile the flight plan. Finally, the immigration people arrived and stamped our passports. The New Zealand station telexed in the latest weather, and we taxied out gingerly, with our heavy load of fuel and leaking strut.

Leg 8: Guadalcanal to Darwin

There was no control tower (just a remnant of the military tower from the war), so there was no ground or takeoff clearances to get; just taxi out and take off. The runway was fairly short, and with our heavy load of fuel, I needed all the runway I could get. To use every inch, I held the brakes as the engines ran up to full power, then released them. We made it with several hundred feet to spare, although we then had to struggle to clear the mountains after we turned toward Darwin.

After takeoff, we were required to make HF radio contact with Port Moresby Radio in New Guinea; if we couldn't, our clearances and overflight permits would be cancelled, and we would have to turn back. Considering the quirkiness of our HF communications, I worried that we might have to make an overweight landing on a leaky landing gear strut on the short runway back at Guadalcanal. The HF gremlins were not harassing us today. Port Moresby heard us loud and clear.

The GPS satellites were not so accommodating. As predicted by the Trimble charts, we had good navigation readouts only for the first two hours. After that, we were reduced to dead reckoning, just like the most basic small aircraft. Then Port Moresby told us that Gurney beacon, a key fix to check our position, was out of order. The clock and the compass were to be our only navigational tools today. But I wasn't too worried. It would be fairly difficult to miss the continent of Australia altogether. And there would be some landmarks along the way: a few islands south of New Guinea, the Great Barrier Reef, and Cape York Peninsula.

Still flying above and through clouds approaching Cape York, we were flying by dead reckoning—without any navigation input or ground checkpoints whatsoever—as we

Guadalcanal — Darwin

Equator

Guadalcanal,

Darwin, Australia

AGGH	Guadalcanal, Sol. Is.	09°25.25'S	160°03.19'E
ADDN	Darwin, Australia	12°25.82'S	130°53.62'E
	1,980 miles	192 mph	10:20 hours

had for almost 1,000 miles (the distance from Miami to Washington, D.C.). N76TT hummed along, blissfully unaware of the vast expanse of water below it and how little its pilot knew of its position. After almost five hours of flying by faith and compass, we sighted our first checkpoint—Thursday Island, off the tip of Cape York Peninsula. At last, after hours of reporting estimated positions to Port Moresby and then Brisbane Control, we had a positive fix. Surprisingly, we were only a few miles off course, and right on schedule. Once again, the winds had stayed on our tail, as they had all the way from San Francisco. My decision to fly east to west, it appeared, had been a good one.

As we flew on across the Gulf of Carpentaria, the satellites came back above the horizon and we started getting GPS readouts. Even better, for the first time on the entire trip, HF radio reception was perfect, perhaps because of the equipment used by Australia's Northern Defense Area. We got a simple, direct clearance on into Darwin. The setting sun nearly blinded us during the approach, but we touched down smoothly.

We had conquered Earth's largest ocean, and we were nearly halfway home.

4

"We'd already flown from Europe
to America, and I really wanted
to fly across Africa.**"**

Night falls quickly in Darwin; the sun that had blinded us on approach was swallowed up by darkness as we cleared customs. The Aussie inspectors were friendly and efficient, although extraordinarily picky—one even unfolded a wadded-up gum wrapper in Fran's purse to check for contraband. We then taxied over to the Darwin Aero Club, where we were greeted by Langdon Rogers, a best friend from Miami who had moved to Sydney and flown up to Darwin to meet us. Langdon gave us a traditional Aussie welcome: he climbed up on the wing with two cold beers. A bunch of his new-found flying mates were waiting for us inside, and as you might expect, the tops of a lot of cold Foster's lagers were popped that night in celebration of friends reunited and a milestone accomplished.

The next several days were set aside for more serious matters of maintenance. The landing gear strut needed repair. The engines needed an oil change and a 50-hour check that included cleaning the fuel injector nozzles and spark plugs. These tended to plug up and foul from dirty, leaded fuel, which was so common in the South Pacific. Fuel poured from barrels seemed to cause the most problems.

Darwin Maintenance Service did the job quickly and

at a reasonable price—except for the fuel and oil. I was by now accustomed to high fuel prices, but the oil price of more than $8 a quart came as a shock. Since each engine took 12 quarts, the cost of the oil change was $200, not counting labor. Knowing that I'd soon be heading into some pretty off-the-beaten path places in Southeast Asia, India, and Africa, I bought an extra 24 quarts to take along, just in case. My total bill for oil came to $400—cash only, please.

Darwin lies in Australia's desolate Northern Territories, at the top of the Outback. We are glad to have a few days off to relax after our Pacific crossing and see this beautiful area. We take a two-day trip to Kakadu National Park, the highlight of which was a boat tour along the Yellow River. This area defies the dry and dusty image of the Outback; it's more like the Florida Everglades than a desert. We see hundreds of birds with such wonderful names as cockatoo, darter, rainbow bee eater, jabaru, lily trotter, kookaburra, and pygmy goose. The huge salt-water crocodiles are too close for comfort—my comfort, at least.

In Kakadu we also see cave drawings, Aboriginal rock art, and termite mounds seven feet high. We spend the night at a hotel operated by the Aborigines and shaped like a huge crocodile. We celebrate the Fourth of July with a dinner of grilled kangaroo and "bug meat" (white grubs). Ugh!

Leg 9: Darwin to Bali

Our stay in Australia ended on Saturday, July 7, when we took off for the next leg of our journey, to Bali, Indonesia. As we checked out of the hotel to leave for the airport, we got some good news: permission to fly into Thailand had finally been granted. Fortune was smiling on us, for it was the last possible moment we could have gotten the approval—and without clearance through Thailand, we would have faced a grueling 1,700-mile nonstop flight from Singapore to Colombo, Sri Lanka, the next planned stop. Now that we had the okay from Thai authorities, we could make the more direct 1,300-mile hop across the Bay of Bengal from Phuket, Thailand.

For the flight to Bali, we donned for the first time our official-looking pilot uniforms, which were decorated with colorful, impressive-looking patches. We'd been advised that Asian and African functionaries would be impressed by such militaristic plumage, however meaningless, and that our passage through their bureaucratic gantlets therefore would be much easier.

Because the GPS satellites were not in favorable positions, we didn't leave Darwin until almost noon. As we taxied out for takeoff for the six-hour flight to Bali, we were the heaviest we'd ever been. Full tanks and the extra cases of oil didn't help. The tower wanted me to make an intersection takeoff on the short general-aviation runway. But I knew it wouldn't be enough at our weight, so I asked to use the long 10,500-foot main runway instead. It took 15 minutes to taxi all the way to the end of it.

As I pushed the throttles forward, the engines, with their freshly cleaned plugs and nozzles, seemed strong. We climbed out with both the HF radio and the GPS system working flawlessly. Our clearance took us along airway Gulf 642 direct to the Bali FIR. But when we switched over from Darwin to Bali, the HF reception went to pot. We heard nothing from Bali, and had no idea whether they heard us or not. The only thing we could do was to report our position in the blind and hope for the best.

Out of the blue, I heard a British Airways jetliner giving a position report. BA pilots always refer to themselves as "Speedbird," a holdover from the old days when the airline was called BOAC [British Overseas Airways Corporation] and carried the insignia of a bird. As I'd done back in San Francisco with the American Airlines jet, I decided to use the commercial jet as a relay station. As I called him, I was tempted to say "Hello Speedbird, this is Tweety Bird," (I was getting a bit of a complex about always being the only small plane way out there among the big guys) but thought the better of it. In any case, the pilot cheerfully relayed my position report to Bali.

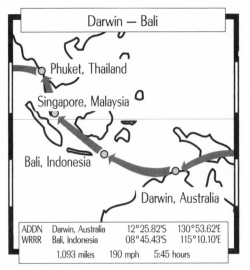

About 150 miles out, I was able to tune in the ATIS [automatic terminal information service], a recorded message that continuously gives current weather and runway information. Unfortunately, because of the thick accent on the tape, I couldn't understand much of it. The wind was from *grmlptsshtrm* at ten knots, and planes were landing on runway *gzrnpltz*.

When I switched over to the tower and started talking to a human being, things weren't much better. English is supposed to be the universal language of aviation, but I could hardly understand a word he said. I asked for a descent from 8,000 to 3,000. The answer was unintelligible. Finally, about two miles out, I just said, "N76TT cleared to land on Runway 9, is that affirmative or negative?" The reply, at last, was comprehensible. "Affirmative, N76TT."

Taxiing in after landing, I feared I might have some explaining to do about why I'd failed to understand the approach instructions and not gotten a landing clearance until I was only a mile from the runway. Sure enough, several official-looking military vehicles drove toward us with lights flashing and we were signaled to park away from the main ramp area. Three Indonesian officials in full uniform got out, rushed over to the plane, stepped up to our open cabin door, and reached in to shake our hands in congratulation. The accompanying soldiers stood rigidly erect at attention with their attack rifles resting on their shoulders.

They eagerly asked all about the round-the-world flight, requested decals and stickers (which I gave them) as mementos, and saw to it that we were ushered through customs and immigration in about five minutes, rather than the five hours we'd been warned about by other pilots. Our uniforms seemed to be working.

Our cab driver wants to take us to a nearby tourist beach hotel, but I had done my homework, and tell him to take us to the Kupu Kupu Barong bungalows in Ubud, about an hour and a half away. My research is accurate—it turns out to be a beautiful place overlooking a rushing gorge of the Ayrong River, with fabulous views of rice paddies, palm trees, and exquisite gardens. We instantly fall in love with the place—perhaps one of the most beautiful hotels in the world!

The six days we spend there are a wonderful blur of exotic food, Legong dancing, baskets, fresh tropical fruits, carvings, the Monkey Forest, ducks, people carrying anything and everything on their heads, temple offerings, incense, music, motorbikes, and more. I'll never forget the people—especially the happy shouts of the kids splashing in the river below us, and the sweet, graceful

soft-spoken girls who serve our food. ("Please enjoy your meal.")
Tom and I often joke about delaying the trip and just staying there
for a few months to "find ourselves," like the hippies of old.

One evening in the room, we are startled to find a fat, two-
foot-long lizard crawling about. When Tom calls the front desk, he
is told that it is a gecko, known to bring good luck to those whose
house he had chosen to inhabit! With half the world left to cover
in the Cessna, we decide we had better just get used to him.

Gecko luck didn't help us much with the Balinese
bureaucracy back at the airport. Going through all the formalities—forms, forms, and more forms—took better than an
hour. It would have taken much longer without the help of
our ground handler, Dewa Gede Mgursh Swastha, who
smoothed the way for us by smiling, cajoling, and slipping
dollar bills into the appropriate pockets. He turned out to be
an air traffic controller as well, and he spoke the same kind
of marbles-in-the-mouth English we'd heard on the way in to
Bali. It was just the way Indonesians speak our difficult language.

The fees we were charged were outrageous. Despite the
fact that we'd already paid $600 to the dispatching service
back in Houston for prearranged ground services in Bali, we
were charged $205 for ground handling, $49 for general fees,
$32.40 for navigation, $49.71 communications fee (I hoped
they'd spend it on English lessons for the air traffic controllers), $11.96 landing fee, etc., etc. But in the end, Bali was
worth the price of admission.

At least I didn't have to buy gas there. By cleverly filling the tanks back in Darwin, I still had plenty of fuel left for
the next leg to Singapore, thereby avoiding another Balinese
ripoff. It wasn't until we got to Singapore that I learned that

Bali gas was by far the cheapest of any of the 20 landing places on the trip. (Indonesia, in fact, is one of the world's largest oil exporters.) My cleverness had cost me hundreds of dollars.

After filling out all the forms and paying the fees, we were driven to the surprisingly modern briefing room, where we filed our flight plan and looked over sophisticated satellite weather analyses. Finally we had permission to walk out to our plane. Next stop, Singapore.

Today is July 12th, a Thursday. In one month we'll be home.

Leg 10: Bali to Singapore

The takeoff and departure went smoothly, but it wasn't long before we ran into a heavy storm. The raindrops pounded the windshield with a steady roar, and the turbulence made the Cessna shake, rattle, and roll. But after a while we broke out into clear, smooth air to the sight of a hundred-mile plume of dust and brown smoke streaming from the crater of "The Mountain of Fire," one of many volcanoes on the island of Java. Crossing the Sea of Java north of the island, we looked down on mystical islands and lagoons. We were indeed a long way from home.

HF radio communication with Singapore was lousy, so we ended up relaying our position reports 2,000 miles back to Darwin Control, who then forwarded them ahead to Singapore. A roundabout method, perhaps, but it worked. Finally, as we neared the Malaysian capital, we were able to establish contact on the VHF radio. The Singapore controllers spoke better English than their Balinese counterparts, but I still had some trouble understanding the clearance to

Horsba. I had never heard of a six-letter fix. The controller painstakingly recited the phonetic spelling—Hotel-Oscar-Romeo-Sierra-Bravo-Alpha—several times. I simply couldn't find it on my chart. (It turned out that the DOD chart I was using didn't show Horsba intersection.)

Our destination was Seletar Airport, which is a joint military/general-aviation field about eight miles north of the main international airport. The weather was poor, which worried me, because Seletar was a VFR-only airport, with no instrument-approach procedures for bad weather. If I couldn't see the runway as I flew over the field, I would have to divert to the big, busy international airport, where landing fees were prohibitively expensive to discourage little guys like me.

The Singapore controller gave us radar vectors direct to Seletar, meaning that the controller, monitoring my position on his radar screen, simply told me which direction to fly and when to turn, relieving me of any responsibility for my own navigation. Fortunately, I was able to catch a glimpse of the runway through the murk, and was able to land VFR.

After landing, we were advised to turn off to the right. Big mistake. There were no customs facilities in sight, so we made a quick U-turn and taxied back across the runway, where the marvelously quick and efficient customs people handled us with dispatch. Singapore is that kind of place—very well-organized and efficient. The cleanliness and sense of order were very impressive. I did not expect to like this modern city of skyscrapers very much—particularly after experiencing the mystical natural beauty of the South Pacific—but I found myself drawn to its vibrancy and energy. I'll be back someday.

We get up early and wear our flight uniforms to breakfast where we get plenty of stares. Tom has a good steak and I eat light. Our taxi barges through the morning traffic to the military base where Seletar Airport is located. Dozens of military aircraft are parked around the hangar with signs saying "NO PHOTOS."

Tom goes to the apron control office to pay fees and arrange for fuel. They have a neat gravity-fed gizmo for fueling planes from above, still Tom is dripping wet from the heat and sun by the time he gets back from the tower. We take off at 11:25 A.M. into clouds and patches of rain. We both keep our pencils and paper ready to listen for instructions, which come fast and furious,

and to take notes. What an adventure this is!

Leg 11: Singapore to Phuket

The short 600-mile hop from Singapore to Phuket, Thailand, was routine at first. Instead of messing around with the stubborn HF radio and relaying messages through Darwin, we were able to communicate directly with a series of ground controllers on standard VHF frequencies. We cruised over beautiful Kuala Lumpur and the glorious islands off the west coast of the Malay Peninsula. Entering Thai airspace, we climbed to 12,000 feet. By the time we got to within 50 miles of Phuket, I figured it was time to start a descent for landing. As I picked up the mike to ask for clearance to a lower altitude, Bangkok Control, in a burst of static, went dead. The

71

GPS tracked our progress as we closed in on our destination—40 miles, 30, then 20—still at 12,000 feet. Finally, the static cleared and Bangkok came back on the frequency. They cleared us for an immediate descent to 3,000 feet.

I hate rapid descents, because the air-cooled engines lose their heat very quickly when their power is reduced and the cold air rushes through the nacelles. This "shock cooling" can cause the cylinder heads to contract suddenly, warp, and eventually crack. I didn't like treating my engines this way, but I had no choice. I gritted my teeth, closed the cowl flaps to reduce the flow of cooling air to a minimum, and pulled back the throttles as much as I dared. When I lowered the landing gear and flaps, we began to drop like a rock.

As we passed through 6,000 feet, the tower operator described VFR weather conditions below the cloud deck. He

cleared me for the ILS 27 approach into Phuket. Wow! That was fast! A new problem: I had no plate, or chart, for this particular approach. My DOD charts listed only an NDB approach to Phuket, which the operator curtly disapproved, so I had to figure out the ILS 27 approach myself. I confirmed the ILS frequency with the tower, and somehow managed to latch on to the ILS signals, and into Phuket we went, uneventfully.

Since Phuket lies near the notorious Golden Triangle drug-smuggling area, I figured we'd meet a swarm of customs, immigration, and security people who would go over us and the airplane with a fine-tooth comb. But to our surprise, no one seemed to be around. We waited and waited for the armored cars to arrive, but no one paid us the slightest attention. We walked from one end of the terminal to the other, but it was deserted. Finally, someone waved us over to an ancient little fire station, where we found one rusted truck and a group of men sitting around playing cards. No one spoke English; they simply motioned for us to sit and wait.

The ever-impatient Fran came up with the best idea of the day. "Why don't we just go back to the plane and start unloading our luggage?" she said. We did, and just as we turned the key to lock up the plane, an official car drove up and took us to an enormous terminal on the other side of the airport. After an hour of paper shuffling, we changed some dollars into bhats, grabbed a taxi, and endured a hair-raising 45-minute ride to a little seaside hotel in the town of Patong Beach.

Next morning we call home and talk to Tiffany, Tom, and Michael. We always find this a difficult process, partly because of the unfamiliar and sometimes primitive phone systems, and partly because the calls make us very homesick for them. During most of the trip, our minds are so occupied by flying and struggling to adjust to entirely new cultures every day that our "real" lives at home sometimes drift to the back of our minds. But when we hear their voices over the scratchy phone lines, the emotions come rushing back, and we miss them terribly.

Phuket really comes alive at night. Picture a 100-yard-long street lined with 40 bars—that's about one bar every fifteen feet. Each one has five or six young girls enticing passersby to come inside, and more girls roam the streets searching for any males who might be seeking the pleasures of their company. At one place, we see a small elephant standing at the bar, eating peanuts and drinking beer just like any other patron. Not exactly our style, but it is all part of this round-the-world adventure.

We did not dally to taste the pleasures of Phuket. We had the Bay of Bengal to cross. But our destination was not to be Colombo, Sri Lanka, as originally planned. Before leaving the States, we had spent hundreds of dollars and many hours of planning to get reservations, clearances, permits, and fuel in Colombo. The civil war in Sri Lanka, an island-nation just off the tip of India, made the bureaucrats there skittish about foreigners, and we had great difficulties with all the permits and clearances.

What finally stymied us was the fuel situation. Although jet fuel was plentiful, the only aviation gasoline to be found in Sri Lanka was at a small general-aviation airport about 30 miles away from Colombo International. It would have been no problem to hop over there and fill up with avgas. But there was a Catch-22. That airport had no customs or immigration office, therefore we would have been required to fly back to Colombo to be rubber-stamped out of the country. With a full load of fuel, we would be more than three-quarters of a ton heavier than the plane's maximum allowable landing weight. Anything less than a perfectly smooth landing back at Colombo might damage the landing gear. Since I had never before landed the plane at anywhere near that weight, the odds were against a perfect "greaser" touchdown. I decided it wasn't worth the risk. So it was no-go to Colombo, and all our planning and effort to get the approvals and clearances had gone down the drain.

Our new destination would be Madras, India, about

400 miles north of Colombo. The diversion to Madras would add more than 300 miles to the 2,000-mile next leg to the Seychelle Islands, off the coast of Africa. We had already flown nearly 2,400 miles nonstop over water between San Francisco and Hawaii, and we figured the 2,300-mile hop from Madras to the Seychelles would be a piece of cake. Madras it was.

We wanted to get to the Phuket airport early. We made arrangements with the taxi driver who brought us to our hotel to meet us again at 7 A.M. He was right on time. At the airport we went through all the usual bureaucratic hassles and paid the usual outrageous fees. I roused the fueler from a nap in the shade underneath his truck, and had the tanks filled. Once again I crossed my fingers hoping that the gas was high on octane and low on water or dirt. "Pay in cash, U.S. dollars," he said in the only English words he knew.

Leg 12: Phuket to Madras

It was almost noon by the time we got our clearance to Madras and taxied out for takeoff. It was a great feeling of freedom and release to leave all the bureaucracy and form-filling behind and head out over the vast blue Bay of Bengal, where there wouldn't be anyone to bother us for more than a thousand miles.

About halfway across, we ran into one of the infamous monsoons common in this part of the world. Fortunately, from inside the cockpit, it seemed like any other moderate rainstorm. We cruised on uneventfully until the Madras controller began radar-vectoring us into position for an ILS approach. He apparently wanted to practice giving headings. He had us turning first right, then left, then right, then right some more, now left, then left again into a heavy rain shower. For 20 minutes he kept it up. I didn't mind. In fact, after so many days of flying across huge empty spaces all alone, it comforted me to know that now there was a controller sitting in a big dark room somewhere watching me track across his green screen, guiding me through the air-traffic labyrinth.

Finally he cleared me for the ILS approach, just as a long runway stretching out ahead of me appeared through a break in the clouds. But something was wrong. As I headed for the runway, the localizer needle was swinging wildly off-center. Trained to believe my instruments instead of my eyes, I banked the plane to follow the needle. My training paid off. It turned out the controller had lined me up with the main runway at a nearby military base. Had I tried to land there, I might well have been shot down—or at least impounded for a while. We landed in Madras (at the right airport) after seven hours, 15 minutes.

I was exhausted by the flight and the five hours of bureaucratic battles that had preceded it. All I wanted to do was park the plane, grab a taxi to a nice comfy hotel, and hit the hay. This being India, it took almost five more hours to satisfy the officials.

We'd been told to park at the old terminal, but customs and immigration were two miles away at the new terminal. A couple of eager ground handlers drove us to the new terminal, where we cleared customs and immigration and changed our money into rupees. Then came the trudge back to the plane to supervise the refueling. But the fuel-truck driver said he took only dollars. We, of course had just changed all of our ready dollars into rupees. (Our long-term stash of dollars was hidden behind the instrument panel, but I figured if I made a spectacle of retrieving it, everyone within miles would soon know where they could find 20 years' income.) He finally agreed to fill the tanks and then accompany us back to the new terminal, where we would change our rupees back to dollars and pay him. But the fueler wouldn't accept just any dollars. A slight tear or smudge was grounds for rejection. He carefully wrote down the serial number of each bill he accepted while I fumed in frustration and fatigue.

The ground handlers then announced that their fee would be $454. (No wonder they had seemed so eager!) I informed them that there must be some mistake. I was a Cessna 310, not a Boeing 747. They brought out their official book that showed they charged the U.S. Air Force planes, no matter what the size, $1,287. Hey, I told them, the U.S. Air Force can afford it; they're used to paying $5,000 for toilet seats and $300 for screwdrivers. But I was not the U.S. Air Force.

I had been advised by a veteran international pilot back in Miami to always be humble and self-effacing during entrance formalities in far-off, third-world countries. But, he'd said, there were times when you just had to rant and rave. I decided this was

one of those times. Instantly changing back into my blistering old self, I let them have it. It worked, to some degree. A supervisor was summoned, who agreed that since we were carrying no passengers or cargo, and were just passing through, that maybe half that amount—$227—would take care of our bill. And, he said, the fee would also cover any ground handling necessary for our departure.

I thought that even $227 was outrageous, but I doubted he would reduce the amount much more, and I realized we might never get out of India if I made him angry. I paid.

Our introduction to the extreme poverty of India began even as we left the airport. A frail, handsome young boy tried to help us carry our luggage, but we were traveling so light—just a couple of small handbags—that I refused his entrepreneurial offer. But after seeing how wretchedly poor the people of India were, I later regretted not being more compassionate. (Months later the incident still bothered me.)

The taxi ride to the Taj Hotel in downtown Madras greatly exceeded any danger we had experienced over the ocean. As life-threatening events go, a mere sputtering engine in a tiny Cessna a thousand miles from the nearest land mass couldn't possibly compare to the chaotic traffic, honking horns, swerving, braking, and near-crashes among the cars, trucks, buses, bicycles, rickshaws, and cows of rush-hour in Madras.

We didn't plan to stay long in India, but a general strike the next day maroons us at our hotel. All businesses are closed, and motor vehicles are barred from the roads in sympathy with the Tamils and their war for liberation in Sri Lanka. Mostly we stay in the room just unwinding, reading, and catching up on trip paperwork. We go for a short walk in the vicinity of the hotel, and it leaves us depressed and exhausted. It is hot and the air is choked with dust and pollution. Run-down buildings, broken sidewalks, dust, dirt, and litter are everywhere. Green plants seem hardly to exist. Three goats hungrily tear the paper off a billboard. I know that India "grows" on some people who like to relate fascinating stories about its trains and rivers. I don't think it will ever grow on us.

We arose at 2:45 the next morning, hoping to get off the ground by 6 A.M. for our 12-hour flight to the Seychelles. (Such an early departure was necessary because the airport there, in the town of Victoria on Mahe Island, had no lights, and we had to arrive before dark.) We got to the airport about 4 A.M. The terminal was chaos—people sleeping everywhere, dirt, filth, and pungent odors. Turbaned money changers snoozed on the floor beneath their teller windows. (Did they even have homes?) Down darkened hallways we staggered to pay the landing, parking, navigation, and communication fees. Security officials, barely awake, asked for endless forms and money. We had to step over 14 bodies just to get into the briefing room. At one point, we were startled by gunshots outside the terminal. Turned out they were scaring birds off the runway.

The last straw occurred when a customs official escorted us out to the airplane and discovered that the security seals he had placed on the doors, to detect anything being loaded or removed, were missing. I imagined us being carted off immediately to jail, but after a heated debate the official let the matter slide.

Finally, at 6:30, just as the first hint of light showed in the eastern sky, we cranked up the engines and called for our clearance to the Seychelles. We were told to stand by. We waited. And waited. Finally, to conserve fuel, I shut down both engines and we just sat there. The tower called to ask if we were having trouble.

"Negative, just don't want to waste fuel while I wait for my clearance," I told him. He told me he wouldn't issue the clearance until I had taxied to the end of the runway and was ready for takeoff. (At U.S. airports it's customary—and in some places required—to remain at the parking spot until the flight plan clearance has been received.)

We started up the engines again and slowly taxied the mile and a half to the departure end of Runway 7. As promised, we got our clearance, but were told to hurry into position for takeoff, since there was a plane due to land in 15 minutes. If we didn't take off pronto, we'd have to wait for him. (This controller would have a nervous breakdown in the tower at Miami's airport, where typically two planes land every three minutes.)

Leg 13: Madras to Mahe

With the addition of our new souvenirs, we once again were setting a new record for takeoff weight. (Fran likes to shop, you know.) We rumbled into the air, turned right to 170 degrees, and then intercepted the 185-degree radial from the VOR on airway Alpha 465. We were heading south along the coast toward Sri Lanka.

When Madras Control handed us off to Colombo, the new controller immediately demanded my clearance number. I obediently recited the number, which had been given to me months before back in Miami during the planning phase of the trip. Perhaps because I was two days behind schedule and was merely overflying Sri Lanka rather than landing there, as originally planned, the controller refused to accept it.

I was ready with Plan B. Other pilots had advised me, if I ever got into a situation like this, to simply read off a long string of bogus numbers in a confident manner. I think I used the day's date backwards. Whatever it was, it seemed to work. It got very quiet on the radio. Waiting for his reply, I snapped pictures of the northern tip of Sri Lanka where the thousand-year religious war between the Tamils and the Sinhalese had recently flared up.

Suddenly a new controller came on frequency. In an urgent voice, he shouted, "Aircraft calling Colombo Control, what is the nature of your emergency? What is the emergency? Report your position immediately!"

I wasn't sure if I understood him correctly, so I asked him to repeat. I then replied calmly that there was no emergency, that we'd simply been handed off from Madras Control on the way to the Seychelles.

"November-Seven-Six-Tango-Tango, state your emergency and Air Force identification!"

"Negative, negative, Colombo, we are a non-military aircraft on Airway Alpha four-six-five proceeding to Dabar fix."

"N76TT, turn immediately to two-seven-zero degrees! You are in a prohibited danger zone! Turn to 270 degrees. State your commander's name, country, and postal address!"

Again I told him I was not military, that I was a Cessna 310 on a round-the-world flight, en route to the Seychelles. Once again, he asked for my address. I gave it to him, figuring I had probably ignited an international incident by spying over a war zone. At least I hadn't been shot down yet.

Finally, Colombo told me to switch over to Bombay Control on the HF radio. I repeated over and over "November- Seven-Six-Tango-Tango calling Bombay Control. November- Seven-Six-Tango-Tango calling Bombay Control. Come in Bombay." I sounded like a pilot in one of those 1930s "B" movies about a plane lost in bad weather. But no one ever replied. Rather than switch back to Colombo, I just kept flying. Apparently that was the last anyone on the ground knew or cared about our existence in that part of the world. Frankly, that was just fine with me.

On and on we flew over the Indian Ocean, past the spectacular atolls and crystal-clear water of the Maldives. One by one, the islands disappeared, and soon we were again flying over open ocean. The GPS was working flawlessly, and I dearly hoped it would continue to do so. The Seychelles are nearly 1,000 miles from any other land mass, and we didn't have enough gas to reach an alternate airport. We had only two landing options: the Seychelles or the sea.

The U.S. military keeps a close watch on the Indian Ocean, with numerous ships and several radar antenna atop

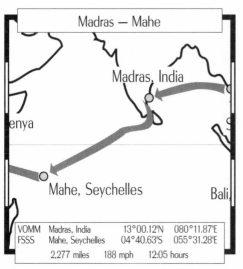

the highest peak in the Seychelles. I wondered how many Navy radar observers were silently watching us as we proceeded across their radar screens. When the GPS told us we were 100 miles out, I gave the Seychelles a call on the radio. To my great relief, they replied immediately. At last, someone officially knew our whereabouts again. And we were right on schedule; there was still more than an hour of daylight left.

Now I had some more bluffing to do. I had not managed to get official permission to land in the Seychelles, despite requesting visas and landing permits months in advance while back in Miami, as well as more recently in

Singapore and Thailand. But no one asked me about permits, so I just landed normally as if I had permission. It turned out to be no problem at all. The authorities on Mahe were very friendly and all the formalities, including fueling up for the next leg to Nairobi, took less than an hour. Talking with the fueler, I mentioned a Seychelles-registered Swearingen Metro turboprop, SY-007, that my friend Bill Dee purchased and had delivered to Miami. He remembered the plane well.

It was dark by the time we finished at the airport. Exhausted from the long day, we tried to hail a taxi to a hotel, but discovered there wasn't a cab in sight. In fact, there was nobody around at all, save for a young woman telephone operator working an ancient switchboard in the terminal. Luckily, she befriended us, and made a hotel reservation and called a taxi for us. It was actually fun trying to communicate with her in the local Creole dialect, a combination of French and English.

We endured a 50-minute ride over steep, winding roads, and then collapsed into bed at the hotel. It had been a long and stressful day—the 2:45 A.M. wake-up, the frustrating departure formalities in Madras, the hassles with the Sri Lankan controllers, and finally the hours of incommunicado flying over the Indian Ocean. We'd spent 12 hours and five minutes in the air, and about seven more hours making arrangements on the ground—just another 19-hour workday.

The next morning, as we lolled around the hotel recuperating, we got a telephone call from the airport: "Move your airplane." It was a long ride back, but not knowing what the circumstances were, we took a taxi back immediately. It turned out to be no big deal; a large four-engine British Navy search-and-rescue jet called a Nimrod (actually a military version of the Comet airliner) had landed the previous night and parked in front of N76TT. Now it was about to leave, and the airport manager feared that the Nimrod's jet blast might damage our small Cessna. Although his fears were unfounded, and they could have easily moved the plane themselves, it was thoughtful of him to notify us.

The next day we headed for the U.S. Embassy in the islands' capital "city" of Victoria. We were a bit worried by recent troubles in Kenya; a tourist on safari had been killed by bandits, and demonstrators in Nairobi had been protesting against Kenya's dictatorial president, Daniel arap Moi. Some earlier U.S. State Department advisories had suggested that Kenya should be avoided.

The alternative was to head north through the Persian Gulf area. (This was just before Iraq invaded Kuwait, so the area was relatively calm at the time.) That route would take us on through the Middle East, Europe, and across the North Atlantic. That was the normal route most pilots followed, but I didn't want to do things the normal way. Besides, we'd already flown from Europe to America, and I really wanted to fly across Africa.

Leg 14: Mahe to Nairobi
We studied the latest advisories and talked to the people at the embassy, who seemed slightly more relaxed about Africa. (And you never know what can happen in the Middle East.) So on July 26 we took off for the 1,311 mile flight to Nairobi.

Years ago, when Tom was planning this trip, he realized that no one flies across Africa to get around the world. So he decided that's what he wanted to do. That was the challenge he needed. So here we are, at last on our way to Africa! There is a lot of weather, and Tom is busy working all the time. I try not to think about the whitecaps below us. Tom is so happy, and I can see he is loving every minute of this.

We finally get a glimpse of The Dark Continent as we reach the coastline of Kenya after about four and a half hours. The broad white sand beach between Mombasa and Lamu is a welcoming sight, and the wide river we see winding below must be the Tana. How exciting it is to fly over brown and green again after so many hours of only blue beneath our wings!

As we flew on toward Nairobi, the terrain gradually rose to almost 6,000 feet. Our destination was Wilson Airport, a small general aviation field nearby. (Once again, the main international airport had only jet fuel, so we had to divert to a smaller airport that served propeller-driven planes.)

We were cleared by the Kenyan controller for an ILS approach to Runway 6. My approach plate for Wilson Airport indicated that not only was there no ILS to Runway 6, there wasn't even a Runway 6! (There was a Runway 7.) I insisted that I didn't want an ILS to 6, which apparently was for Nairobi's big international airport. He insisted, in thick Swahili-accented English, that I accept the approach. I insisted I wouldn't, and said that I was unfamiliar with the air traffic control system in Nairobi. (I later found out that the customary approach to Wilson is to shoot the

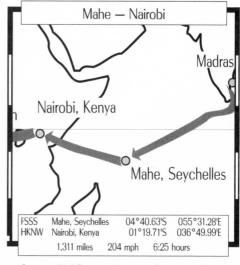

FSSS	Mahe, Seychelles	04°40.63'S	055°31.28'E
HKNW	Nairobi, Kenya	01°19.71'S	036°49.99'E
1,311 miles	204 mph	6:25 hours	

85

ILS to the international airport, and then break off toward Wilson at the outer marker.)

Finally, a new controller came on the line, this one British. He quickly understood the problem and vectored me over to Wilson. Just as I was turning and switching frequencies to contact Wilson tower, Fran shouted. "Look out! There's a plane flying right at us!"

Before I could react, it was by us. Whew, that was close. Then, suddenly we saw another Cessna 310 passing right overhead. I slowed up to let yet another 310 get in front of me in the pattern. Planes were everywhere, seemingly without control from the ground, taking off and landing on runways that crossed each other. The tower cleared me number two to land, so I just followed the other 310 in, my head swiveling constantly all the way down in search of other planes.

When the wheels finally touched, I felt a great sense of relief, but also one of foreboding. At last we had reached Africa, and the most challenging, frustrating, and dangerous part of our round-the-world journey was about to begin.

5

> **"**This was 'it.' This was what I had been working toward for the past three years... it wouldn't get better than this.**"**

Our welcome in Nairobi presaged the frustrations that were to come. After touching down on the runway, I couldn't get any clear instructions about where to park, so I just kept following the other 310 that we'd followed in to land. We lucked out. He stopped at customs parking. I needed a few minutes to relax after the stress of the long flight, the approach mix-up, and the near collision, but the Kenyan officials descended upon us immediately. We weren't quite sure whom to listen to. One guy told us to move the plane over to Safari Air, which was our prearranged contact. So we parked right in front of their office. Then another guy told us to move it over into the grass. Rather than unlock the plane, remove the sun-screens from the windows, and go through the whole start-up routine, I asked a group of Kenyan men hanging around if they'd help me just push the plane over there. Without hesitation, they jumped to the job. It went well, and everyone turned out to be very friendly.

I also had a mechanic check the nose fuel tank, for I had smelled gas fumes during a previous takeoff, and worried that there might be a leak. I also wondered why I'd been able to get only 20 gallons out of what was supposed to be a 30-

gallon tank. They drained the tank, and sure enough, it turned out to be just a 20-gallon tank instead of the advertised 30. In a way, I was relieved. Instead of having 46 gallons of unusable fuel, I had only 36. All along, N76TT had been carrying 60 pounds less weight than I'd thought.

Wilson Airport resembled a huge Cessna fly-in. Cessnas of every description were parked all over the field. Small planes are the primary means of transportation within Kenya, and the C-310s like ours and the slightly larger 400 series Cessnas are extremely popular. We got many offers to buy our plane. People were always shoving business cards at us, inquiring politely if we'd gotten fed up yet with all the bureaucratic hassles and red tape, and were perhaps ready to return to Miami by airliner.

They were right about all the hassles. Going to Miami via Europe would definitely have been the easy way home. But I don't always do things the easy way. I was determined to follow the equatorial route across Africa. We planned to cross the entire continent in one fell swoop, flying nonstop from Nairobi almost 2,000 miles to Libreville, Gabon, on Africa's west coast. Along the way, we would pass over some of the wildest and most primitive countries in the world: Tanzania, Rwanda, Zaire, Congo, and Gabon. The 800-mile stretch across Zaire would be particularly nerve-wracking, due to the impenetrability of both its jungles and its bureaucracy.

Voyager is the only other small aircraft, that I am aware of, to have crossed Africa nonstop along the equator. *Voyager* is the long-winged plane that Dick Rutan and Jeana Yeager had flown around the world nonstop in 1986. Even though they never landed in Africa, they had the same enormous difficulties obtaining overflight permits. (By coincidence, we were carrying the very same NOAA EPIRB that

Voyager carried.) The pilots in Nairobi I talked to—including a grizzled veteran of the Aero Club of East Africa who'd been flying around The Dark Continent for decades—had never heard of anyone doing it or wanting to do it.

Despite the many months of planning the flight back in Miami, we had managed to obtain overflight clearances only for Kenya and Congo. We had much better luck in Nairobi, however. Safari Air was miraculously able to get us overflight permits for Tanzania, Rwanda, and Uganda. Air Service Gabon, at our destination in Libreville, got us the permit for Gabon.

The only missing link was Zaire—a chaotic, almost Stone-Age country of vast jungle ruled by a despotic dictator. The old-timer from the Aero Club warned us that if we ran into mechanical problems over Zaire and were forced to land, we should not—he emphasized NOT—try to survive. "Just nose the aircraft over," he demonstrated with his hands, "and dive straight in. That's much preferable to finding yourself injured in the middle of an impenetrable jungle or, worse yet, falling into the hands of the Zairian government!"

Safari Air was unable to get us an overflight permit, so we approached the Zairian Embassy in Nairobi ourselves. We spent innumerable hours in the crowded, primitive hole in the wall they called an embassy, befriending an employee there with smiles, compliments, and baksheesh in the form of crisp American $20 bills. After some persuasion, he agreed to send a telegram to the capital city of Kinshasa, 1,700 miles across the jungle at the western end of the country.

I wasn't so sure there was a telegraph line across the country. Months ago, Fran had sent a letter and then several telexes requesting a permit number. She had sent another from the South Pacific. I had sent one as well. None had been answered. We would have phoned or faxed, but there was apparently no phone number to call. We had even tried various American embassies, but were disappointed to find they refused to help peons like us.

For six days, we visited our new "friend" at the Zairian Embassy, and for six days we heard nothing. In his broken English, he couldn't promise us that a permit would even come through at all. We had no choice but to begin our other preparations for the flight and hope for the best.

I went out to refuel the plane, but was told that to buy fuel for a foreign-registered aircraft such as ours, one had to pay in Kenyan schillings certified to have been exchanged at the Central Bank of Kenya, which was their equivalent to our Federal Reserve. At sunrise the next day—24 hours before our hoped-for departure—I went to the Central Bank. It was a madhouse. At a nearly empty office serviced by eight employees, we were directed to a small room, serviced by one employee. It was full of perhaps 50 anxious people, just like us, who were all, apparently, trying to obtain some sort of official certificate or approval. After more than an hour of waiting in the crowded "line," pushing and shoving constantly to hold my position, I finally reached the window, where I was told that it was the wrong window. I should go up to the second floor.

We went to the second floor, where, after another hour's wait, a functionary informed me that I did not need a certificate of exchange, that I could buy fuel with money changed at any bank. Barely controlling my rage, I asked if an officer of the Central Bank would please call the fuelers at the airport and tell them that. To my surprise, it was done.

Then it was back to the Zairian Embassy for the umpteenth time, where we were told that a copy of the telegram they had sent to Kinshasa might be available that afternoon, and that he would try to persuade the Ambassador to sign it for us. I could not make him understand that what I needed was a simple permit number, not a copy of a telegram requesting clearance, even if it was signed by an ambassador. The air traffic controller in Kinshasa, or wherever he was, didn't care about ambassador's signatures—all he wanted was a permit number.

On to the airport, where the plane was fueled. At one point, fuel being pumped into one of the cabin tanks too fast spurted out and drenched me from head to toe. Reeking of fuel, I then walked more than a mile to the fuel office to pay the bill. Then came the landing fees. And the parking fees. And the departure fees, which couldn't be paid without first getting the signatures of the tower operator and the weather man.

More cash flowed over at Safari Air, but I didn't mind paying, since they'd been wonderfully helpful. I paid telephone and permit fees, plus a maintenance bill for a 50-hour check that included a compression test and the cleaning of the plugs and fuel injector nozzles.

Then back to the infamous Zairian Embassy. We sat and waited. And waited. And waited. The 5:30 P.M. closing time approached. Finally, at 5:28, we were handed a copy of a telegram that requested "permission to transit" Zaire. It had not the slightest look of authority to it; even the ambassador's seal was unimpressive. Our entire trip hung on this unreal-looking, flimsy piece of paper that may or may not have been received by the proper authorities. It perfectly summed up Zaire. It is a country of regulations piled upon regulations, all written in such a way as to obscure their true meaning, thereby wringing the maximum amount of baksheesh out of foreigners. We were out of time. The stamped copy of the telegram would have to do. I figured if a Mirage jet fighter of the Zairian Air Force intercepted us, I would wave the piece of paper at him through the window.

We headed back to the airport for one last signature. One would think that after all the frustration and delay, we would harbor ill feelings toward Kenya, but the opposite was the case. We had to remember, after all, that it was the British who set up these bureaucracies in the first place. The native Kenyans now in charge of them were always more than courteous, polite, and helpful. Their friendliness, laughter, and dignity overwhelmed us.

I certainly could do without this day. There is so much to see and do in Nairobi, but we must keep our priorities straight, and number one is to be ready to leave by tomorrow. Tom needs me for support, and I decide to grit my teeth and make the best of it. We go back and forth between the city and the airport four times. I wait in taxis while Tom waits in offices. (It's almost impossible to find a taxi, so we don't want to give it up once we flag one down.) I get a lot of time to read and visit with the locals. I learn from the taxi driver about tribal rivalries and the recent political demonstrations.

I watch traffic jams, throngs of people, and double-parking chauffeurs. In spite of the obvious poverty in which they live, many people dressed in white shirts with ties, and conduct themselves with a dignity I find poignant.

At last, the formalities are finished.

I spent a restless night, tossing and turning. For the first time on the trip, I had real concerns about our safety.

Zaire had a reputation for quick, angry reactions to infringements of its airspace and regulations. Had the telegram been received? Had the right people in the Zairian air-traffic system and Air Force been informed? Would I even be able to establish radio contact with Zairian controllers on their notoriously unreliable equipment? Would we be mistaken for an enemy intruder and shot down, or forced to land and rot in some Zairian jail?

And then there was the matter of the terrain. In a way, the jungle was worse than the ocean. We stood a reasonable chance of surviving a ditching at sea; we had a life raft, and could be rescued by a boat or ship once our location was known. But putting the plane down in the jungle would be far more dangerous. We would have to glide into the treetops 100 feet up, and then tumble down to the jungle floor. If we survived that impact, we'd be in the middle of the largest untracked jungle on the planet. Even if by some miracle someone heard our emergency beacon, there would be no way to reach us. We would be truly marooned in a vast, fetid sea of green undergrowth. (Bold warnings on our charts emphasized that "positions are approximate, data incomplete, no assurance of exactness ... maximum elevation figures are believed to be correct.")

A third factor worried me as well: the short runway at Wilson Airport. It was only 4,800 feet long, shorter than any runway we had ever taken off from with a full load of fuel. It would force me to use a dangerous takeoff technique that I'd never had to use before. My normal heavy-load takeoff procedure was to lift off at an indicated airspeed of 106 knots, which provided a safe margin above the stall speed and minimum-control speed. This technique, however, resulted in a takeoff roll of over 6,000 feet. To get off the ground in 4,800 feet I would have to lift off sooner, at less than 90 knots—a dangerously slim margin above the stall and minimum-control speeds.

(Stall speed is the slowest speed at which an aircraft can fly. Any slower, and the wing loses lift suddenly and the plane plummets. For a normally-loaded Cessna 310, the stall speed on takeoff is 77 knots, but at our weight, it would rise to 86 knots.)

(Minimum control speed, or V_{mc}, is the speed below which the plane could roll over uncontrollably if an engine fails. The 310's normal V_{mc} is 80 knots, but ours would be higher—by precisely how much, I couldn't determine.)

Our takeoff speed would thus be within a few knots of both the stall speed and V_{mc}. There was virtually no margin for error.

To make matters worse, the field elevation at Wilson was 5,549 feet. The thinner air at this altitude robbed the engines of power and the wings of lift. We would have only about 75 percent of the normal maximum power available for takeoff, and N76TT would have to get rolling along the runway faster than normal just to get flying speed through the thin air. Warm temperatures would thin the air even more and further sap our performance. So, we decided to make our takeoff in the cool air of dawn.

Starting a year ago, back in Miami, I had on dozens of occasions double-checked and triple-checked the 310's performance charts to calculate N76TT's theoretical takeoff roll under the expected conditions at Wilson. After all the figuring and calculating, again and again I came up with the same number: 4,670 feet. If the charts were correct, our margin for error was 130 feet—less than three percent.

I certainly hoped the Cessna performance charts for

the 310 were indeed correct. Many lightplane performance charts, unfortunately, are crude at best. They are often based on rules of thumb, estimates, and extrapolations, not real testing. Performance figures are often exaggerated to boost sales. But I had flown hundreds of hours in N76TT, carefully comparing its actual real-world performance to the book figures, and I had found them to be accurate as far as they went.

The only problem was, they didn't go far enough to cover our takeoff from Wilson. Cessna publishes takeoff-roll numbers only for weights up to 5,500 pounds, the original maximum gross weight. At our extreme overweight condition, all bets were off. So I had to come up with my own figures by extrapolating the Cessna figures for various lower weights. I did this by simply extending the curve on the graph of weight versus takeoff roll.

I honestly am getting very tired of hearing about the whole takeoff thing. Still, I knew that's one of the ways Tom accomplishes his goals—he talks about them. A lot!

I also consulted with local pilots, who had a lot of real-world experience flying out of this airport in overweight 310s (although not as overweight as we would be). The consensus of the locals was that with luck I could make it, just barely, as long as we took off in the cool air of early morning. Once the sun came up and the temperature started rising, we wouldn't have a chance.

Amid all this uncertainty that was running through my head that night, there was one more kicker—a 12-foot-high fence just off the end of the runway. Built to keep the zebras, gazelles, and giraffes from adjacent Nairobi National Game Park off the runway, it would be a formidable obstacle

95

for an overloaded plane barely staggering off the end of the runway. Local pilots advised me to leave the landing gear down and flare over the fence, mushing back down on the other side and bouncing the wheels on the savannah if necessary. But I decided to raise the landing gear as quickly as possible, to reduce drag and tuck the wheels up a few precious feet higher as we passed over the fence.

Tom is totally preoccupied with the takeoff from Wilson Airport. He talks to everyone he can about it, hoping to pick up any tips that might add to our safety. A couple of days before the takeoff, we even walk out to the end of the runway and check the ground conditions, picking up any rocks we find. Tom figures we can gain a few precious feet by starting with the main wheels off the end of the runway, with just the nose wheel on the asphalt. Instead of picking up rocks by the runway, I wish we could spend this limited time sightseeing and shopping.

Our wake-up call came well before dawn, but of course I was ready for it, not having slept a wink all night. We arrived at the airport before the sun and watched the comedy begin. People began arriving about 6:15, and at 6:30 the wheels started and the doors were unlocked. We went through the usual bureaucratic gantlet, filling out forms and running back and forth to get required documents and signatures. Finally, we seemed to be done, and picked up our little bit of hand luggage and began walking toward the plane.

But a security officer told us we couldn't do that. I would have to leave Fran and the bags behind, walk to the plane myself, and then taxi over to a certain white stripe on the pavement, where the luggage could be loaded aboard. After a very thorough preflight inspection, I cranked up the engines in the cool, still dawn. The engines surged to life, as if they too were eager to get on their way over the jungle that lay ahead. N76TT felt very heavy as it lumbered over to the white line. But the ordeal wasn't yet over; another inspector started asking us questions about the luggage, where we were going, and so forth. The stress and the frustration were just too much for Fran, and she began to sob.

I just want to get on with it. I know every minute counts, because the longer we wait, the warmer it gets, and that means the takeoff will be even more dangerous. When the last inspector keeps asking those stupid questions, my sniffles turn to sobs. Tom stays calm, but I am just a pack of emotions.

I am so keyed up I can hardly breathe. The feeling is complex; fear and exhilaration all mixed up together. Will we crash trying to take off from Wilson field? Will we breathe 15 minutes from now? Will I see our children again? I put us in God's hands.

Leg 15: Nairobi to Libreville

I taxied slowly out to the runway, got my en route clearance, and then permission to take off. I took a deep breath, for I knew this was the most dangerous takeoff I had ever attempted. I took my time, carefully taxiing through the rockless grass off the end of the runway that Fran and I had surveyed days before. I threaded past the runway lights, bouncing over clumps of weeds and thick grass until I was able to turn around and line up with the runway. I nudged the nose wheel onto the asphalt and rolled forward until the propellers were just over the end of the runway. (I didn't want them kicking up any dirt or pebbles when full power was applied.)

I double-checked all systems. Engine instruments all

in the green. Magnetos checked, props checked and full forward in fine pitch, trim set, aux pumps on LOW. I rehearsed the takeoff procedure in my mind. I would leave the flaps up at first to reduce drag during the initial roll, then lower them ten degrees for extra lift just before rotating. I'd leave the elevator neutral until just before liftoff, again saving a few pounds of drag.

With feet on the brakes, I pushed the throttles slowly forward until they wouldn't budge anymore. The engines roared and the plane shook. I carefully set the mixture to a fuel flow of 118 pounds per hour, which would give us maximum power at this altitude.

It was all-or-nothing time. With engines screaming and adrenaline flowing, I released the brakes. The plane surged forward and the main wheels bumped onto the pavement. Slowly the airspeed indicator came to life, and we rolled straight as an arrow down the white line in the center of the runway. As we passed the cross-runway, the airspeed was 63 knots. I reached for the flap lever. I felt the wings beginning to lift, and the weight was coming off the wheels. Seventy-six knots now. Not much runway left. I could clearly see the 12-foot fence at the end of the runway, and the herds of animals beyond it. By now, it was too late to abort the takeoff; we were committed to go. My eyes were very wide, because I still wasn't sure we'd make it.

As we scream down the runway, here I am, stuffed in the cramped little cockpit, trying to lean forward to help the plane's balance, holding the Nairobi charts on my lap with my right hand, and reaching awkwardly back with my left hand to keep the en route charts on top of the tank behind me from sliding back where we'd never be able to reach them. All the while, of course, I am wondering if I am going to die in the next few seconds.

The airspeed indicator now read 80 knots. The fence was rushing toward us. Eighty-five knots indicated. I pulled gently back on the yoke and N76TT, like the lady she is, lifted off ever so gently just as the red runway end lights passed beneath her wheels. The

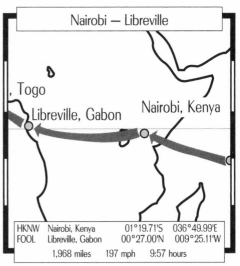

fence still loomed ahead. I nudged her up a bit and hit the gear-up lever. She struggled up out of ground effect (the supporting cushion of air near the ground) as the wheels began to retract. I almost closed my eyes as we skimmed over the fence, the retracting wheels clearing it by what seemed to be inches to spare.

I was happy to be alive.

We were not out of danger yet. We were mushing along barely 20 feet over the ground, as wildebeests, antelopes, and giraffes scattered in all directions. Until we picked up more speed, we were unable to climb any higher. I prayed that a giraffe would not stray into our path, for I wasn't sure we could have cleared him at that moment. For the next few moments, any power loss on either engine would send us instantly spinning into the ground in a huge fireball.

After a few seconds, N76TT began to gather speed, and we inched our way higher. Within about 30 seconds, we'd reached 110 knots and were climbing at about 350 feet per minute—a rather anemic climb rate, but at least we were going up! As we pulled away from this beautiful, vibrant, and complex land and headed toward the Great Rift Valley and the lofty mountain range of central Africa, I felt totally exhilarated by events of the moment.

This was "it." This was what I had been working toward for the past three years, perhaps since I was 17 flying around in the Piper Cub. Whatever motivated me to conceive and execute this trip, I knew it wouldn't get better than this.

Ahead of us lay six African countries and 10 hours of difficult flying through unknown weather over impenetrable jungles. To make matters worse, radio communications with Nairobi Control were very difficult. Reception was poor and we were continually being asked to report our position and estimated arrival times at various compulsory reporting points, some of which were not on my chart. To make matters even worse, both engines were running a bit rough, probably due to spark-plug fouling caused by excessive lead in the "green" fuel I'd bought in Nairobi. It was tense and complicated flying, but the beauty of this country was so overwhelming that Fran and I were happy nonetheless.

Our first border crossing is into Tanzania. As we near Tanzanian airspace, we see the villages of the Masai Mara below us and, up ahead, Lake Victoria, similar in size and shape to Lake Okeechobee back home in Florida. Victoria is the largest lake in Africa and the source of the Nile River.

We got our clearance into Tanzania with no problem and cruised on across Lake Victoria with good radio communication. Soon thereafter, the terrain began to rise, then plunged down into a huge canyon—the Great Rift, a valley that runs for thousands of miles down central and southern Africa, created by the crunching together of the earth's crust.

I knew the Rwandans had a reputation as sticklers for rules and clearances, so I worried that if there were some foul-up with our permit number, we wouldn't be able to bluff our way through, as we had done in Sri Lanka. Instead, we would be ordered to land and our plane would be confiscated. Therefore, I was quite relieved when the Rwandan controller in Kigali accepted our permit number and cleared us through his airspace. One more obstacle out of the way.

The tiny country of Rwanda—home of the famed Gorillas of the Mist—is next. Can the wonderful gorillas see us? Can they hear the unfamiliar sound of our engines? On we fly for many lonely hours. Below is just endless green jungle. I visualize our small plane crash-landing in the dense jungle and our being eaten by animals or tied to the stake.

The terrain began rising once again, and soon we saw the 14,800-foot peaks of Africa's tallest mountain range poking up through the clouds. We also flew through dark smoke from fires that are continually set to clear fields in this part of the world. After about 20 minutes, we had crossed most of Rwanda and were approaching the border city of Goma, Zaire. I was instructed to switch frequencies and contact Zaire Control. I got nothing but squeals and static. Repeated calls brought no response.

Should I hesitate and hold at the border, I wondered.I decided to keep going. We crossed the border into Zaire!

Meanwhile the weather was deteriorating rapidly, and we were soon flying through sporadically heavy rain. As we flew in and around the showers, we'd occasionally break out into the clear, and I would look down briefly at a carpet of green jungle that seemed to stretch into infinity. Then I'd blink and get back on the instruments. The engines were still running rough, and I tried not to think about what would happen if we had to crash-land down there.

Further tries at radio communication with Zaire Control were futile. I decided to forget about the radio, permits, clearances, and despotic dictators, and just concentrate on my flying. It was too late to turn back, and I figured the Zairian interceptor pilots wouldn't want to fly in this weather. There was certainly no other civilian air traffic within hundreds of miles, so we weren't likely to run into anybody.

The Zairian navigational beacons were no better than their communication radios. As we droned across the jungle, we discovered that every single NDB listed on the chart was inoperative. Our only link to civilization was the trusty GPS system and the four satellites orbiting 11,000 miles overhead. For four hours we flew incommunicado through the rain and clouds over Zaire. Finally, with a great sigh of relief, we crossed over the Congo River (now called the Zaire River) into the country of Congo, the legendary home of Tarzan and Jane. We would not be spending our golden years in a Zairian jail cell after all.

This is incredible! After all the long, frustrating hours we put into complying with their regulations, we won't even talk to anyone in Zaire. It just doesn't make any sense. I'm glad the ordeal is over.

Between the clouds and heavy rain, we could see that the river was huge, much wider than I had expected. Even having crossed the mighty Mississippi a number of times, I was impressed. It seemed a fitting place for the historic meeting of Stanley and Dr. Livingston. I tried to call Brazzaville Control in Congo, but heard only a bit of garbled French and then static. We kept flying.

Congo, like Zaire, was jungle as far as the eye could see. The rain continued to give our plane a free wash. Eight hours after takeoff from Nairobi, we crossed the border into Gabon, whose capital city of Libreville was our destination. It was now only about two hours away. Once again, I tried the radio on many frequencies, both VHF and HF. Once again, nothing. At one point, I heard two people conversing in French, then silence. The rain began to fall harder and harder, beating on the windshield like buckshot. I called Libreville Radio one last time—and heard a faint reply! After five hours of radio silence, we suddenly were in touch with the world again.

I reported my position, and there was a slight pause before the unbelieving voice of the controller replied. Other than *Voyager*, I wondered if he had ever talked to an American-registered civilian plane (signified by the "N" in N76TT), and if he'd ever had anyone report in from so far east. Considering the inefficiency of African bureaucracy, it was unlikely that he was even aware that we were scheduled to arrive.

I tuned in the Volmet recorded weather station and was happy to hear that the forecast for Libreville was good—scattered clouds at 5,000 feet. Where we were, 100 miles to the east, it was still raining hard. About 40 miles out, I contacted the Libreville controllers and got permission to descend to 2,600 feet, although I found their French-accented English hard to understand. (By this point, it didn't matter whether I could understand them or not. I was going to land in any case.)

GPS: 00°10.00'N, 009°25.55'E. We were practically on the equator when cleared for the ILS approach to Runway 16. As we flew over the initial approach fix, the rain and wind were bouncing the plane around like a punching bag. (So much for African weather forecasts.) After the hairy takeoff and 10 hours of difficult instrument flying over the jungle without an autopilot, this was the last thing we needed. Fran, who has flown through a lot of rough weather with me, was very frightened, and I must admit I was a bit concerned myself. The plane rocked violently in the turbulence, and the rain beat on the windshield.

As we got lower and lower, I still couldn't see the runway. Not entirely trusting the African ILS system, I double-checked our progress with the GPS. The glide-slope and localizer needles were swinging wildly back and forth as the turbulence knocked us off course. A wing dropped; I was turning too sharply now. Wings back to level; then I was below the glide slope. Both needles pegged; I was dangerously low and off course. This was no time to be a hero; I decided to abort the approach, go around, and try again. Just as I reached for the throttles to make the missed approach, the needles came back to the center. "I've got it, Fran," I yelled. "We're going to be all right!"

We continued our descent—500 feet, then 400 feet—with still no sight of the runway. Our decision height was 310 feet; if I didn't see the runway by then, we'd have to declare a missed approach, go around, and attempt the approach again. As we neared 300 feet, I could just make out the runway through the rain-smeared windshield. We were right on the centerline and the glide slope, perfectly lined up for landing. In the heavy rain, I could barely see anything straight ahead, so as we settled down to the runway, I looked out the side window.

I pulled back gently on the yoke, and we touched down smooth as silk. A greaser, and just when we needed it most.

The ILS approach to Libreville is wild—turbulent, no visibility at all, and the airport doesn't even have radar to keep an eye on us. But Tom's landing is perfect. He really is the WGA (World's Greatest Aviator). We fly 9 hours and 57 minutes across the heart of Africa. How many hours and days and weeks had we spent mentally and physically preparing for this feat? How many times had Tom flown this leg in his mind? Praise the Lord! We made it!

Now only the Atlantic Ocean stood between us and Miami. We were on the home stretch.

6

"There was the second alternative: just head directly west from Africa to the West Indies."

We were limp with fatigue and relief as we climbed out of N76TT. A local pilot told us we'd landed in the middle of the worst weather in Libreville so far that year. Weather forecasting anywhere is an inexact science, but in Africa you can forget about the science part. It's just inexact.

After the customs formalities, we walked a half mile down the road to the Gamba Hotel and cracked open a couple of six-dollar beers. That's a day's salary for the average citizen of Gabon. If a beer was $6, we wondered what everything else would cost!

Fran and I had imagined that the dollar would buy more in Africa, but we learned it wasn't true. In countries such as Kenya and Gabon that import so many of their necessities from Europe, the cost of living was extremely high, and our dollars wouldn't buy much. In other countries, such as Togo, where more locally-produced products were available, our dollars went further.

Glancing at a newspaper in the hotel, we saw the headline HOLY WAR! Iraq had just invaded Kuwait. If we had taken the normal round-the-world route through the Middle East, we'd have been caught right in the middle of serious fighting—and who knows what would have happened. Our good fortune in choosing the Africa route—and then completing it—deserved a celebration, so we walked three miles to the only good restaurant around. There were no other customers the whole evening, and the chef, who had been the Royal Chef for the last king of Zaire, spent two and a half hours preparing a special seven-course French dinner. It was a fitting, final flourish to our trans-Africa flight.

The next morning, after hot croissants and coffee, we set off to find the International Hotel, where we know a fax machine is available. The head of telecommunications at the hotel is very helpful. He volunteers that he earns $222 a month. We attempt to call the kids (8 A.M. there), but the phones are down. Tom does manage to get through to his office, after which I sense from his mood that all is not going smoothly.

We run into an Englishman who came to Gabon to do a geologic survey for an oil company. He too uses GPS to find his way around the countryside and precisely plot his data. He and Tom rave on about the irony of two people in this remote primitive corner of the world using GPS for such wildly different purposes.

Later, we walk to the airport. Tom sends a telex to Togo and files our flight plan by enlisting the help of several French-speaking pilots.

From Libreville, our route would take us north and west along the bottom of the hump of West Africa to Togo, a tiny country nestled between Ghana and Benin. It would be a straight 700-mile shot across the Gulf of Guinea. I chose Togo as a stopover because Michael Hacker, a friend of mine back in Miami, was Togo's Honorable Consul General, and had given me a letter of introduction he promised would smooth the way for me. Months of trying back in Miami to get a landing permit for Togo had failed, but Air Service Gabon quickly obtained one for us. Even though English is the official international aviation language, I now believe that landing permit requests in English end up in the circular file in many non-English-speaking countries such as Togo.

Leg 16: Libreville to Lomé

After the usual departure formalities, we taxied out and took off for Lomé, the capital of Togo. The weather had cleared, and the HF reception was excellent. It all seemed so easy compared to what we'd just been through. Lomé picked up our transmission 200 miles out, and all went routinely as we touched down at the big international airport there. We were told to park in front of a Falcon 50—a big three-engine ultra-luxurious business jet—that was sitting on the tarmac. As we pulled into our parking spot, I noticed the Liberian flag on the jet's tail and the guards with machine guns ringing it. I recalled that Liberia was just then in the midst of a huge civil war, with the government under siege from two rebel factions. So this is where they're hiding the president's plane! The Togonese people were friendly and helpful, and we got through the landing formalities quickly. I didn't even have to pull out my letter of introduction.

The next day we set off on foot for the local Saturday market. It is a colorful swirl of sights, sounds, smells, and a bewildering variety of items for sale. From sardines to cashew nuts in old liquor bottles to voodoo objects—it is all here. Ladies carry trays piled high with food on their heads. Men in Muslim turbans and long white pajama-like gowns sell swords and leather boxes. As we make our way through the crowds, we obviously stand out as foreigners. The locals are constantly trying to get our attention:

"Madam, look what I have for you!" Groups of three or four women huddle around, plaiting one another's hair into hundreds of tiny braids. One asks me if she could go to work on my long hair, but I tell her I am not quite ready for a new look.

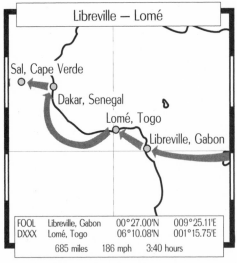

Sunday we attend a beautiful church service in the main cathedral. The vivid colors and joyful singing make for a very uplifting experience. When it comes time for the collection, ladies holding plastic bowls sway in the aisles to the beat of the music while the people go up to drop in their coins. (Tom makes a contribution, too.) It is wonderful to see the generosity of these people, most of whom were very poor.

Later, at a service in English, prayers for peace in Liberia are offered. Many refugees are in Lomé to escape the strife caused by the current Liberian civil war. "In just one week," I whisper to Tom, "we'll be back in Miami."

Our next leg would take us to Dakar, Senegal, at the very westernmost end of Africa, which would be our jumping-off spot for the flight across the Atlantic Ocean. The direct route from Togo to Dakar would have taken us across Ghana, Ivory Coast, Guinea, and Gambia—a bureaucratic nightmare of permits, clearances, and radio frequency changes. I decided to try to beat the system. I would instead take a roundabout route that simply followed the coastline around to Dakar. By flying well offshore over international waters, I figured I would avoid the communications and navigation charges, checkpoints, reporting points, and all the other hassles. I could simply turn off my radios and cruise peacefully to my destination, without bothering anybody or anybody bothering me.

Leg 17: Lomé to Dakar

I didn't even file an IFR flight plan. For the first time, I was going to fly VFR, which meant I could fly wherever I wanted to as long as the weather was reasonably good and I had at least three miles visibility. And, presumably, I wouldn't have to talk to anybody. (At least that's the way it works back in the States.)

It didn't happen here. Shortly after takeoff (which I had delayed till just past 6 A.M. to beat the fee for using the runway lights), we headed straight out over the ocean, where we would then turn right to follow the coastline. But Lomé Departure Control ordered me to contact Accra Radio in Ghana. That's pretty much the way it went for the next 1,700 miles—everybody wanted to get into the act, and I ended up having a very busy day of reporting points, estimates, and new frequencies.

For a short time, however, I lost radio contact just 10 miles off the Liberian coast. I tried diligently to re-establish contact—really, I did—but nothing worked. So Fran and I broke out our box lunches of sandwiches and fruit and cruised along without a care in the world.

Soon we heard another aircraft, VVJM, calling on the frequency. By listening in on the conversation, we learned that Victor-Victor-Juliet-Mike was a U.S. Navy transport flying into Freetown, Sierra Leone (the country north of Liberia), to pick up Americans fleeing the vicious civil war then raging in Liberia. In fact, we later learned that nearly a hundred people had been killed that very day—not 10 miles from where Fran and I cruised by peacefully munching our sandwiches.

On the same frequency, I then heard a controller calling, "N76TT, this is Freetown Radio." My better instincts told me not to reply (I was flying VFR and, strictly speaking, wasn't required to), but I figured it would be a good idea to have somebody know I was out there in case of an emergency. So I replied. Sure enough, it was a mistake. "N76TT, please state the aircraft owner's full name and address." As I'd expected, all they wanted was to send me a bill for communication and navigation services.

After flying more than eight hours, crossing 1,730 miles, and talking to nine countries, we entered the Dakar FIR and reported in. We were cleared for a visual approach to the international airport, but three miles out, dust and haze obscured the runway. A mile out, however, the runway appeared, and we made a rough landing in the blowing dust and sand. We taxied a mile to a parking area that was about as far from the terminal as it could be. A few curious workers came by to see what a little Cessna was doing out there on the edge of the Sahara Desert. We gassed up, and then came the endless arrival formalities.

We took a taxi into town, which was about eight miles away. The taxi seemed older than I felt by now, and sure enough, along a particularly lonely stretch of road, bang, a tire blew. I figured the driver was going to rob us—it would have been very easy for him—but he simply went about his business and changed the tire. He didn't try to rob us until we got to the hotel, demanding a fare that was double what we'd been told was the normal rate. After changing some dollars, I handed him half of what he had asked, and he accepted it without argument. It turned out that bargaining is the normal way of doing business in Senegal. Virtually everything in the country is marked with a very high price, but it's quite easy to negotiate a lower one.

The next day we immerse ourselves in this bustling city. Setting off on our own tour with a map torn out of a guidebook, we ride the local buses, eat lunch on a sidewalk surrounded by horribly crippled people bowing in prayer, visit the national museum, and get drenched in a rare desert downpour. Among other items, the local hawkers try to sell us watches, soccer balls, and a huge gaudy gold mirror that had a built-in clock decorated with unicorns.

Dakar was our jumping-off spot across the Atlantic, but the question was, a jumping-off spot to where? The shortest route from Africa across the Atlantic was to Recife, Brazil, nearly 2,000 miles. Back in Miami, I had originally planned in some detail to use this route, starting from Abidjan in the Ivory Coast. But by the time we reached Africa, I was eager to get home.

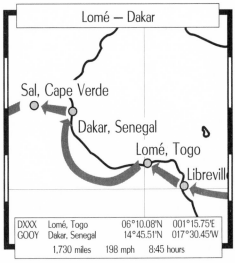

The extra couple of days it would take to jog far south and then work our way back north along the coast of South America didn't look too appealing. Moreover, several pilots had warned me never to land in Brazil, because of the common practice of delaying transient aircraft for the purpose of extracting huge bribes for fuel and permits. Atop everything else, I was feeling a compelling need to return to my real estate business, which I had learned through phone conversations required my earliest presence.

By the time we got to Libreville, I had decided to skip the Brazil route and fly across the North Atlantic from Dakar. That still left two alternatives. One was to head north to the Canary Islands, then up to the Azores, across to Newfoundland, and then back down to Miami. The longest over-water leg along that route was "only" about 1,600 miles, but it was a very circuitous route that would add several days' traveling time. Plus, it wasn't exactly the equatorial route that I wanted to take. And we'd already done the Newfoundland-Miami route twice. I wanted to explore new territory.

There was the second alternative: just head directly west from Africa to the West Indies. Barbados was an English-speaking country, not known for bureaucratic obstinacy, and from a previous visit there I remembered the people to be most friendly. It was just under 3,000 miles away, and I figured if we had no headwinds, we could just make it. But "just make it" is not the sort of phrase one wishes to think of when embarking across the Atlantic Ocean. I did not want to bet my life on a tailwind.

Looking over the chart, I noticed the Cape Verde Islands, a small archipelago 400 miles west of Dakar. We could use them as a stepping-stone and cut the over-water leg to Barbados to less than 2,600 miles. That would give us a safety margin I could live with. I had heard of the islands, and knew that they were a spawning ground for hurricanes, but that's all I knew about them. Was there an airport there? Was the runway long enough? Did they have aviation gasoline?

A quick check of my navigation charts revealed that the island of Sal in the Cape Verdes had an airport, and that the runway was almost 11,000 feet long—plenty long enough for us, even with the heavy fuel load. A pilot's handbook I carried stated that aviation fuel was available, but I had no way of knowing what kind. I decided we would simply have to fly out there and find out.

With the help of Base Ops back in Houston, we were able to get a landing permit for the airplane. Then we went down to the Cape Verde Embassy in Dakar to see about a visa for us. "It'll take eight to ten weeks," the smiling man behind the desk told us. Once again, I decided we wouldn't let these bureaucrats keep us down. We had gotten this far around the world, and we weren't going to let a little thing like lack of a visa stop us now. We would take off, fly to Sal, land with no visa, and just see what happened.

Leg 18: Dakar to Sal

Next morning we launched for Sal, a two-hour flight through a slightly sandy haze. Along the way, we heard the Navy plane Victor-Victor-Juliet-Mike again. In fact, when Dakar radio couldn't hear one of our position reports, VVJM relayed the message for us. As we approached to land at Sal, the island looked as desolate as the moon. No green here. Only sand dunes and rocky, rolling, barren hills. We touched down on the huge runway, and as we climbed out of the plane and started walking toward the small terminal building, I expected the worst.

To our astonishment, the local officials were very

friendly. They were amazed that we had arrived without a visa, but it was no problem. We could stay as long as we liked. But, if we didn't mind, the security police would keep our passports in a desk drawer in their office until we left. That was all there was to it.

We still faced a major hurdle: fuel. I found the fuelers, and my heart sank when they told us that there was just one small tank of avgas on the airport, and that the rules prohibited its use for international flights. They simply were not allowed to sell it to us. After a long discussion, it was agreed that perhaps I could take up the matter with the airport's top official. I hinted that I might be willing to provide certain financial incentives to the official. I was instructed to return the next morning.

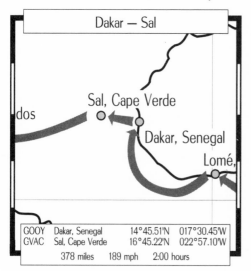

GOOY	Dakar, Senegal	14°45.51'N	017°30.45'W
GVAC	Sal, Cape Verde	16°45.22'N	022°57.10'W
	378 miles	189 mph	2:00 hours

Fran and I grabbed a taxi to a nearby hotel. To our surprise, it turned out to be a small, charming place filled with young, wealthy, sophisticated Europeans. We had apparently stumbled onto some sort of secret jet-setters haven. Although we were mere "prop-setters," we enjoyed ourselves immensely. There was one group of Americans, though: the young and tanned crew of a huge, magnificent yacht anchored offshore, whose owner was there to catch the world's biggest marlin. Dinner was spectacular, the ocean marvelous.

The next morning we arrived at the airport bright and early. Always the optimist, I proceeded as if we would get the fuel. We retrieved our passports and filed a flight plan the likes of which I'm sure had never been seen here: "Sal direct Barbados." I got the latest weather, which was a hand-drawn and colored map with realistic clouds as they would appear along our route. Very impressive, but the only problem being that it had been drawn the night before by a 16-year-old art student who had no idea of what kind of weather we would encounter. I handed out official-looking NOAA decals to everyone in sight. Everything was ready, except for the fuel. Now it was time to check on that situation.

We finally located the fuelers. They had good news. The Minister of Transportation had decided, in view of our worldly needs, to let us have the fuel we required. Moreover, there was no need of any financial incentive, and we had his sincere wishes for good luck on our journey. Then the fun began.

After a long wait, the gas cart finally appeared. It was 18 years old and came equipped with a wooden-handled hand pump. To make a long, hilarious story short, it took two and a half hours and five people, including me, to pump the 100 gallons needed to top off N76TT. (In the States, it would take three or four minutes to pump that amount.) If anyone could have seen this Rube Goldberg operation, they would surely have thought it a comedy skit in a made-for-TV movie.

By the time the job was done, my flight plan had expired and had to be refiled. I briefly considered postponing the flight until the next day, because our late departure would probably get us to Barbados after dark and Cape Verde was fun. But I figured we had the momentum going, the weather looked decent, and we'd probably better get out of there before some reason was found to detain or delay us.

As we rolled down the runway for takeoff, I knew we were facing quite a challenge. The 2,446-mile distance to Barbados was longer than the Oakland-Hawaii leg, and we would be completely on our own. There were no airways from Africa to the West Indies, no navigation fixes, no helpful American or British airliners cruising overhead to relay messages and keep us company. For virtually the entire leg, we would have no one at all to talk to on the radio, no one to call in case of trouble.

And to make matters worse, for most of the flight, the GPS satellites would be out of position, and we would have no navigational guidance whatsoever. I briefly considered making the flight that night, when the satellites would be in excellent position, but back in Miami I had made a policy decision never to fly over water at night on this trip. In case of an engine problem, ditching at night would simply be too dangerous.

Without GPS, we would have to dead reckon (I never liked the "dead" part of that phrase) across the ocean, basically just aiming the nose at where Barbados was supposed to be, using only a $48 compass for guidance and hoping that the winds wouldn't blow us too far off course.

Nevertheless, I felt confident. We would have at least a couple of hours of fuel reserve, maybe more if we got good tailwinds, and five GPS satellites were scheduled to come back above the horizon toward the end of this leg. Even if I screwed up the dead reckoning, or winds blew us off course, we would at some point get a GPS readout of exactly how far off course we were. (I figured anything less than 200 miles off course wouldn't be a serious problem.) Still, it gave me pause to think we would be dead-reckoning across the Atlantic using exactly the same navigational method Charles

Lindbergh had used 63 years ago—and we'd be flying an over-water leg 454 miles farther than he had.

Leg 19: Sal to Bridgetown

After yet another long, long takeoff roll, we began the slow climb to our usual cruising altitude of 8,000 feet. (Although a higher altitude would let us fly a little faster on the same fuel, I find the lack of oxygen above 8,000 feet or so tends to dull my reflexes and sometimes gives me a headache.) Cape Verde Control almost immediately started asking for an estimate to the first checkpoint—as if it really mattered; there was almost zero chance of meeting any other airplane out there. I told them I was busy flying the airplane and to please stand by. Eventually I got everything squared away, and they got their estimate.

Once we reached cruise altitude, about all there was to do was put the nose on a true heading of 270 degrees and keep it there—at least for a while. But without the GPS for guidance, I had to pay very close attention.

Because I was flying a great circle route, my heading would gradually change, becoming more southerly as we flew along. By the time we approached Barbados, the heading would be 240 degrees—a gradual shift in course of about one degree every 80 miles. Since I didn't know exactly what our groundspeed was, I had no way of knowing precisely when 80 miles had passed. An estimate would have to do.

I also had to keep track of the magnetic variation—the constantly changing but very predictable compass error caused by the fact that the magnetic north pole isn't quite at the same spot as the geographic north pole, or true north. In the early part of the flight, I had to add 15 degrees to the true heading to account for for the west variation. As we flew along, the variation increased gradually to 18 degrees west, then went back down to 12 degrees west by the time we reached Barbados.

Another factor that had to be considered was compass deviation, the inherent error of the compass itself that is usually induced by avionics and metal in the cockpit.

The dead reckoning formula is straightforward, but complex. It goes like this, with everything measured in degrees:

Great circle true course ± wind correction angle = true heading, then

True heading + west (*or* – east) magnetic variation = magnetic heading, then

Magnetic heading ± compass deviation = magnetic compass heading, the final result used in piloting.

To make things even more challenging, I had to do all this very precise flying by hand, without the autopilot. Even though it would engage properly after the "repairs" in Oakland, the autopilot still would not hold a steady altitude, oscillating up and down in increasing climbs and dives until it finally disengaged itself. Even with the altitude function off, the oscillations were excessive. Also, it would disconnect every time I transmitted on the long-range HF radio. The radio's extremely powerful electrical signal would trip the autopilot ON switch to the OFF position. I had flown by hand the entire 26,000-plus miles we had covered so far. Actually, I'd kind of enjoyed it. The hands-on flying had made me feel more a part of the action and had given me a greater sense of accomplishment.

According to the unreliable weather reports, there was a tropical depression to the north of us, and to the south an area of storms that seemed to be developing into a hurricane.

Somebody up there must have been looking out for us, because the weather right along our route was relatively clear and smooth. Although I had no accurate forecast of the wind, my previous weather studies revealed that the prevailing winds along our route were likely to be in our favor—the same easterly trade winds brought Columbus to the new world almost 500 years before. (Equatorial trade winds, in contrast to our familiar prevailing winds across the U.S., North Atlantic, and Europe, have a stronger force nearer the surface than at higher altitudes.) So far on our journey, we'd had extraordinary luck with the winds—they'd been on our tail virtually the entire trip. I hoped our luck would hold just one more time.

We droned on and on, talking to no one, the GPS screen blank. Hour after hour, I concentrated on keeping N76TT precisely on the proper heading, hoping we weren't drifting too far off course. An error of just one degree would put us almost 50 miles off line by the time we got to Barbados. And a crosswind of just 10 mph would blow us awry by an additional 110 miles. I figured by the time the GPS satellites came into position to give us a precise fix, I'd be happy to be within 50 miles.

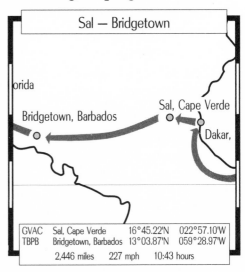

In the past, Tom has been pretty good at dead reckoning. Will he be today? Will the engines keep running? Here we are, out

in the middle of vast Atlantic, alone with the sharks and the hur-ricanes.

As always on these long over-water legs, I mentally rehearse the ditching procedure that Tom and I had worked out:

1. Switch seats with Tom, to put him next to the door.

2. Put on life jacket, snap buckles, but don't inflate.

3. Tie ourselves together with a stout rope. (We'd decided we would either sink or swim together. Kind of romantic, I think.).

4. Tie the grey waterproof emergency bag to Tom's leg.

5. Put the hand-held radio, portable GPS receiver, NOAA emergency beacon, spare batteries, and navigation charts in the bag.

6. Remove plastic cover from the life raft and place the raft on my lap.

7. Place pillow between chest and shoulder harness to reduce impact of ditching.

8. Check that ELT crash beacon strapped to leg is secure.

9. Open cabin door slightly just before impact, to prevent it jamming shut.

It isn't exactly reassuring to be thinking about all this, but at least the seas look smooth down there today. And the water would be warm. If we survived the ditching, we could probably survive for quite a while until somebody picked us up—if anybody even received the signal that we've gone down.

On and on we flew. I was constantly making slight heading adjustments, trying to keep the nose within one half degree of the proper heading. (I'm the meticulous type when it comes to survival.) After about nine hours, the GPS receiver began to blink and come to life. Soon we had a position readout: 14°28.84'N, 55°01.42'W. A quick plot on the chart showed us to be only 29 miles off course! And we were making very good time; the tailwinds had been strong (about 27 knots), and we were just 316 miles from Barbados. There was plenty of daylight left, we had seven hours of fuel remaining, and we had GPS to lead us right to the end of the runway. I breathed a huge sigh of relief—we had it made!

After a while, I called Barbados on the VHF radio. They were astonished to be getting a call from a small plane inbound from Africa, and cleared us into their airspace. The controller spoke with a Caribbean accent, but it was good to hear the familiar professional phraseology I was accustomed to back in the States. Soon, however, the controller began to complain that he could barely hear me because of a gradually weakening signal. So I pulled out my spare hand-held battery-powered radio, and that seemed to work better. We cruised on uneventfully and touched down at Barbados' Seawell Airport. We had successfully dead-reckoned our way through spawning hurricanes and tropical disturbances, and were back once again in the Western Hemisphere.

The last few miles coming into Barbados, I am in awe. There are huge cumulus clouds and small puffs against a sky that seemed bluer than I had ever seen before. The island looks so lush and green. We had been flying 10 hours and 43 minutes, we had crossed the Atlantic, and we were almost home. What a thrill!

We park right under the tower and walk to the terminal. In Barbados, air crew members don't even have to get their passports stamped, but we insist on it—we want proof of this day. After all, how many people can say they've been in Africa and Barbados in the same day? We drop into bed exhausted and have no trouble falling asleep to the sounds of steel drums in the background.

We spend one day resting and sightseeing in Barbados. Ages ago when we were planning the trip, I dreamed of spending days visiting exotic Caribbean islands, but now all I can think of is getting home. We do some exploring, swimming, and visiting the famous Sam Lord's castle, but I am impatient for tomorrow to come.

Saturday, August 11. This is the day I will see my children again after nearly two months! Nothing can go wrong today—and nothing does until we were almost to Miami.

The homestretch flight from Barbados across the Caribbean would be about eight hours, but at least there would be plenty of islands along the way to keep us company. I did an extra-careful preflight inspection of N76TT. The thought of some sort of mechanical problem that might delay us this close to home was too much to bear. But everything looked perfect, and the engines fired up eagerly. Maybe they knew we were almost home.

Leg 20: Bridgetown to Miami

After a routine takeoff we worked our way up through the Windward Islands and then the Leewards. As we neared Puerto Rico, with the U.S. Virgin Islands off to the right, we were entering familiar territory, for Fran and I had flown down here on several occasions. Then on up the Bahamas chain—the Turks and Caicos, the Exumas, Andros Island, and on toward Miami. This was practically our back yard. Fran and I had flown around these islands in our little Ercoupe 20 years ago. The English-speaking voices of the controllers were welcoming and easy to understand. Every time a controller started a transmission with "November..." we would jump, thinking the call was for us. We were still accustomed to being the only November in the sky, but of course back here, everybody had a call sign beginning with November.

Twenty minutes more and we'd be home sweet home. Miami Center cleared us to Eeons intersection, just 30 miles out. "We're almost there, Fran," I whooped excitedly. Then it happened. Miami Center said, "N76TT, hold at Eeons southeast at 6,000 feet. Expect further clearance in one hour."

What was this? We were being put in a holding pattern for at least an hour. I immediately asked the controller the nature of the hold. "N76TT, Miami International Airport is closed." When I asked for clearance to Fort Lauderdale, they said it was closed, too. I felt as if I had just entered the Twilight Zone.

Severe thunderstorms and lightning were enveloping all of south Florida. We listened on the radio as airliner after airliner diverted to Palm Beach, some of them with low fuel after extended holds. In a way, I thought it unfair that after an eight-hour flight we had to hold while the jetliners were being rerouted to Palm Beach after their quick hop down from Atlanta. But then I realized that the flight plan I'd filed listed our 16 hours of fuel aboard.We could hold for another 10 hours at maximum-endurance power settings. The controllers apparently figured we could wait while they took care of the fuel-hungry jetliners first.

It hardly seemed a fitting finale to our round-the-world journey. But I realized we didn't want to land at Palm Beach anyway. We'd miss our welcoming committee and delay the reunion with our kids. Plus, in order to officially qualify for an FAI round-the-world record, we had to land back at Miami.

We circled and circled. It gave me time to worry once again that we might be suspected of drug smuggling. Here we were, flying in from the farthest corner of the Caribbean in a fast twin-engine plane with a fuel capacity of 16 hours.

Would the DEA be waiting for us when we landed? A delay like that would be incredibly frustrating after all we'd been through. Finally, after an hour of circling, Miami cleared us to the Biscayne VOR, and eventually, after a pass over the airport, we intercepted the localizer on the 9 Left final approach.

Then came the words we'd been dreaming about for almost two months: "N76TT, cleared to land." Our Cessna 310 kissed the ground in a perfect landing at 6:57:28 P.M., August 11, 1990. Fran and I kissed the ground when we climbed out.

We weren't finished quite yet. We still had to pass through customs, and there was the very real possibility that we would be searched for drugs. I imagined DEA inspectors unleashing drug-sniffing dogs and disassembling N76TT panel by panel looking for the "sugar bags" we'd undoubtedly collected during our 17-country trip. (It's happened to me many times after flights back from the Bahamas.)

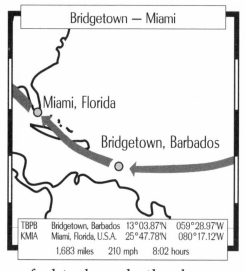

I could also imagine an FAA inspector meticulously checking over all the paperwork for the auxiliary fuel tanks and other long-range equipment. Would he discover that my HF radio was in fact a non-FAA-approved $800 ham radio rather than a $15,000 FAA-approved model? Technically, it was illegal, and might be a plum for a promotion-hungry inspector. (The $800 non-approved one works just as well, by the way.) On top of that, all of our long-range tanks were now technically illegal, too. They had been installed under a ferry permit to leave the country—but no one had said anything about coming back to Miami with them.

Even customs could nab us for all the Japanese-made equipment on board—the HF, the hand-held VHF radio, the camera—which we had failed to register with them before we left the U.S. Without that registration, they could be called in for duty payment. Conditioned by two months of bureaucratic hassles, I was expecting the worst.

We walked into the customs office, filled out a few forms, and returned to N76TT with the customs inspector. The plane, so beautiful and reliable, looked elegant in the fading twilight. I walked over to the nose compartment, lifted the cover and started my spiel, "This is the auxiliary nose fuel tank, and this is some extra oil, tool kit, spare parts...."

He interrupted me in mid-sentence. "Do you have cabin tanks, too?" I nodded yes. "Where's your $25 customs sticker for 1990?" I pointed to the decal on the side window.

"Okay, you're through," he said with a smile. I couldn't believe my ears. He didn't even want to see the gifts, souvenirs, and paintings we'd collected.

In the waiting area near the customs office we drank water from a public fountain for the first time in two months. A tattered newspaper gave us the latest on Saddam Hussein. Savoring the moment, we walked slowly out to N76TT to taxi over to Butler Aviation, where we hoped the kids would be waiting. It was dark now, and our intrepid Cessna sparkled in her triumph. As we taxied, I turned on every light we had, including the landing light, so the kids would be sure to see us coming. We taxied over to our usual parking spot and shut down the engines. The propellers came to a stop for the last time.

Then all hell broke loose. People came running from all directions. Tiffany had made a huge "Welcome Home" sign. My brothers were there, along with my 86-year-old mother. Friends milled about everywhere.

I can barely contain my excitement at seeing everybody again. Joy and thankfulness are bursting from me as we pull into our parking spot at Butler. I see the Welcome Home poster. We run into the arms of our children, family, and friends.

It was a time to celebrate, a time to reflect. I had fulfilled my lifelong desire to just keep going, to see what lay over the horizon. We had made the first flight around the world using GPS navigation. More importantly, Fran and I had looked deep within ourselves and found the strength to persevere and follow our dreams.

Epilogue

> **"**How was your trip around the world?
> Are you glad to be back?**"**

For months after we returned, we received invoices with fancy and official stamps for the communications and navigation services we had received. On the brighter side, several magazines printed articles about our trip around the world. We gave lectures all across the United States and received hundreds of telephone calls, faxes, and letters from friends and interested strangers around the globe

About eight months later, I felt most elated when N76TT was just rolling out from a landing at Palm Beach International Airport and the controller said, "How was your trip around the world. Are you glad to be back?" "I'm glad we're safe, it was a great trip! How did you know?" I asked. "I was stationed in Nairobi a while back and was fascinated reading about your GPS trip around the world. That's sure one beautiful 310."

Acknowledgements

A lot of helpful people made
the trip possible.
These are some special ones.

Charlie Armiger ....Trimble Navigation
Jim Cook...Palm Beach Avionics
Henry "Skip" Culver.........................Geo Flight Computer
Bill Dee...Friend and Associate
Bill Desal...Africair, Inc.
Gus Gonzales ....Miami's Best Mechanic
Russ Gordon ....Trimble Navigation
Michael S. Hacker, Esq. ....Honorable Consul General,
                                                              Togo and Senegal
Ron Hitchcock..Tower Avionics
William Kelly......................................Lakeland Instructor
Caroline Macleod, M.D...................Tropical Medicine and
                                                              Traveler's Clinic
David Martinez...Page Avjet
Buddy Morgan ....Trimble Navigation
Cathy Morgan......................................Trimble Navigation
Phil Paxton ....Pilot
Tom Pentecost...................................Boca Raton Mechanic

Specifications

"That's sure one beautiful 310!"

Aircraft Type: Cessna 310-R

Registration No: N76TT

Physical Data
Height: 10'11.8"   Length: 31'11.5"   Wingspan: 36'11"
Engines: 2 six-cylinder, fuel-injected, 285-h.p. Continental
Propellers: 2 constant-speed, three-blade McCauley

Performance

	Standard	As Modified
Maximum Takeoff Weight	5,500 lbs.	6,875 lbs.
Maximum Landing Weight	5,400 lbs.	5,400 lbs.
Empty Weight	3,575 lbs.	3,680 lbs.
Useful Load	1,925 lbs.	3,195 lbs.
Fuel	160 gals. (usable in wing and tip tanks)	420 gals. (384.4 gals. usable) 1-20 gal. rectangular steel nose tank 3-80 gal. rectangular steel tanks behind front seats; total 240 gals. (all gravity fed)
Range	6.5 hrs., 1,152 NM	16 hrs. @ 24 gph, about 2,700 NM

Electronics
Dual King KX155 NAV COM Transceivers
Dual King Glideslope Receivers
Dual Head ARC ADF Receiver
King ADF Receiver
Marker Beacon Receiver
DME Transceiver
Emergency Locator Transmitter
Transponder Transceiver
Bendix Radar
HF Transceiver, mounted between pilot and copilot seats with power
    unit in nose compartment. Antenna connected to power unit and
    extended from nose to tip of vertical tail.
GPS TNL-2000 Navigator Receiver; permanently panel-mounted.
GPS Portable TransPak Receiver positioned on glare shield. (Both GPS
    receivers could be connected to one external GPS antenna.)

Survival Gear
1   4-man life raft with survival equipment and canopy
1   High-quality water desalinization unit
2   Life jackets with lights
1   NOAA experimental EPIRB; COSPAS-SARSAT Search and Rescue
    Satellite System
2   Hand-held emergency locator transmitters
1   Hand-held UHF transceiver and battery packs

Flight Data
Departed Miami:	June 12, 1990, 6:53:00 A.M.
Returned Miami:	August 11, 1990, 6:57:28 P.M.
Total Elapsed Time:	60 days, 12 hours, 4 minutes, 28 seconds
Total Flight Time:	147 hours, 46 minutes
Distance Flown:	28,587 statute miles; 24,861 nautical miles
Average Speed:	193 miles per hour; 168 knots
Fuel Burned:	3,712 gallons
Countries:	17 (34 customs formalities)
Flight Legs:	20

Itinerary

> **"**It's a mighty little island to find in a mighty big ocean. Good luck, Cessna.**"**

Date	Leg	Distance in Miles Naut.	Stat.	Avg. MPH	Time
6-12-90	Miami–Oakland	2,465	2,835	184	15:22
6-16-90	Oakland-Kona	2,064	2,373	205	11:32
6-18-90	Kona-Christmas Island	1,073	1,234	183	6:43
6-19-90	Christmas Island-Pago Pago	1,278	1,469	190	7:45
6-26-90	Pago Pago-Port Vila	1,225	1,409	188	7:27
6-28-90	Port Vila-Santo	140	161	149	1:05
6-29-90	Santo-Guadalcanal	558	642	188	3:25
7-2-90	Guadalcanal-Darwin	1,722	1,980	192	10:20
7-7-90	Darwin-Bali	950	1,093	190	5:45
7-12-90	Bali-Singapore	880	1,012	169	6:00
7-16-90	Singapore-Phuket	541	622	178	3:30
7-19-90	Phuket-Madras	1,112	1,279	177	7:15
7-21-90	Madras-Mahe	1,980	2,277	188	12:05
7-26-90	Mahe-Nairobi	1,140	1,311	204	6:25
8-1-90	Nairobi-Libreville	1,712	1,968	197	9:57
8-3-90	Libreville-Lomé	596	685	187	3:40
8-6-90	Lomé-Dakar	1,505	1,730	198	8:45
8-8-90	Dakar-Sal	329	378	189	2:00
8-9-90	Sal-Bridgetown	2,127	2,446	227	10:43
8-11-90	Bridgetown-Miami	1,464	1,683	210	8:02
	Totals	**24,861**	**28,587**	**193**	**147:46**

Aerodrome Data

"I would at all times know
my position within 25 meters, my altitude
within 0.1 meter… **"**

Ident.	Location	GPS Readings Latitude	Longitude
KMIA	Miami, Florida, U.S.A	25°47.60'N	080°17.40'W
KOAK	Oakland, California, U.S.A.	37°43.35'N	122°13.29'W
PHKO	Kona, Hawaii, U.S.A.	19°44.18'N	156°03.84'W
PLCH	Christmas Island, Kiribati	01°59.21'N	157°22.03'W
NSTU	Pago Pago, American Samoa	14°20.68'S	170°43.72'W
NVVV	Port Vila, Vanuatu	17°42.93'S	168°19.17'E
NVSS	Santo, Vanuatu	15°31.61'S	167°13.44'E
AGGH	Guadalcanal, Solomon Islands	09°25.25'S	160°03.19'E
ADDN	Darwin, Australia	12°25.82'S	130°53.62'E
WRRR	Bali, Indonesia	08°45.43'S	115°10.10'E
WSSL	Singapore, Malaysia	01°25.77'N	103°52.38'E
VTSP	Phuket, Thailand	08°07.91'N	098°19.76'E
VOMM	Madras, India	13°00.12'N	080°11.87'E
FSSS	Mahe, Seychelles	04°40.63'S	055°31.28'E
HKNW	Nairobi, Kenya	01°19.71'S	036°49.99'E
FOOL	Libreville, Gabon	00°27.00'N	009°25.11'E
DXXX	Lomé, Togo	06°10.08'N	001°15.75'E
GOOY	Dakar, Senegal	14°45.51'N	017°30.45'W
GVAC	Sal, Cape Verde	16°45.22'N	022°57.10'W
TBPB	Bridgetown, Barbados	13°03.87'N	059°28.97'W
KMIA	Miami, Florida, U.S.A.	25°47.78'N	080°17.12'W

Glossary

ADF • Automatic direction finder, a radio receiver incorporating a needle pointing to the direction of a transmitting station such as an NDB or AM radio broadcast stations around the world.

AM • Amplitude modulation radio, a method of adding audio to radio; permits longer-range communication than does FM, or frequency modulation.

"automatic rough" • Imagined irregularities in the sound and performance of the airplane's engines as the pilot's mind plays tricks; occurs most often over water and many miles from land.

avionics • Short for "aviation electronics."

best power setting • A compromise of maximum distance, minimum fuel, and reasonable speed. N76TT's is 58% which equates to 2,300 rpm and 22 inches of manifold pressure at 8,000 feet–10,000 feet altitude.

cleared for approach; cleared to land • The point in the landing sequence where it becomes the pilot's sole responsibility to maneuver the airplane to the runway in bad weather using only its instrumentation.

compass rose • A painted circle with radii pointing to the magnetic points of the compass.

DME • Distance-measuring equipment; the distance measured is from ground-based transmitter to aircraft receiver.

ELT • Emergency locator transmitter; a radio that transmits a beep on 121.5mHz to satellites located above 20° north latitude and to rescue aircraft in the area.

EPIRB • Emergency position indicating radio beacon; transmits anywhere in the world on 406mHz to U.S. and Russian satellites the exact location of an aircraft in distress.

equidistant point • The location at which the distance to destination equals distance to point of departure; see *equitime point* and *point of no return*.

equitime point • The location at which the time to destination equals time to point of departure; winds must be considered; see *equidistant point* and *point of no return*.

FIR • Flight information region, an international control area line at which reporting is compulsory before entering a country's airspace.

FSS • Flight service station, a ground station issuing weather, advisory information, and flight plans for aircraft operations.

GNC • Global navigation and planning charts used to navigate great circle routes as with GPS or dead reckoning.

GPS • Global position system, a satellite-based navigation system using magnetic north as a reference; longitude and latitude readouts are displayed in degrees, minutes, and hundredths of minutes rather than degrees, minutes, and seconds.

great circle route • The shortest distance between two points on the earth's surface; equates to a straight line across a sphere, but does not permit a constant compass heading.

gross weight • The maximum total FAA-licensed operating weight of an aircraft including fuel, oil, occupants, luggage, equipment, and. . . souvenirs.

HF • High frequency radio band of 300kHz–30mHz; HF radio normally allows communications over distances further than VHF.

Hz • Hertz, the measure of electrical frequencies in cycles per second; the prefix "k" indicates "kilo," or 1,000; "m" indicates "mega," or 1 million. Radio is separated into discrete frequency "bands," such as HF and VLF.

IFR • Instrument flight rules governing the flight of airplanes solely by reference to instruments; mandatory when in clouds, or when the cloud ceiling is less than 1,000 feet and visibility is less than 3 miles.

ILS • Instrument landing system, a radio beam allowing an aircraft to be guided to a landing by reference solely to cockpit instruments.

INS • Inertial navigation system, an extremely expensive navigation system used by commercial airlines; subject to human errors.

International Date Line • A theoretical line approximately 180°

east and west of 000°00'00" longitude. Crossing from east to west becomes the next day; from west to east becomes the preceding day.

instrument approach procedure • A mandatory guide, depicted on an airport's approach chart, that permits a pilot to fly to the airport by use of cockpit instruments.

knots • Nautical miles per hour, about 1.15 statute miles per hour; never "knots per hour."

Lambert Conformal Conic Projection • A chart projected as a cone conforming to the shape of the globe, making it possible to plot a great circle route as a straight line. Most charts are Mercator Projections that permit only a rhumb line, constant-heading track resulting in greater distances between points.

latitude • Distance north (N) or south (S) of the equator (at 00°00'00") measured in degrees, minutes, and seconds.

longitude • Distance east (E) or west (W) of the prime meridian at Greenwich, England (000°00'00"), also measured in degrees, minutes, and seconds; home of the Zulu (Z) time zone.

loran • Long range navigation, a ground-based radio navigation system usable over only 10% of the earth; very susceptible to error when flying through rain.

nautical mile (NM) • The distance unit of sea and air navigation, 1.852 kilometers or about 6,076 feet, as opposed to the English-measurement statute mile of 5,280 feet.

NDB • Non-directional beacon; a low frequency (30kHz–300kHz) radio transmitting in all directions.

NOAA • U.S. National Oceanic and Atmospheric Administration.

point of no return • The location at which the fuel on board is insufficient to return to the departure point; winds must be considered; see *equidistant point* and *equitime point*.

runway (numbers) • The magnetic compass heading (to the nearest 10°) of a runway with the third digit dropped; i.e., Runway 9 heads at 090° (east); when approached from the other direction it becomes Runway 27 at 270° (west). Large airports often have dual runways designated with left (L) and right (R) following the number.

time zones • Division of the earth's longitude into 25 sectors named by the letters of the alphabet with "J" omitted. Each sector is approximately 15° wide except for two at the International Date Line equal to about 7.5° each, one for identical times in each of the different days.

transceiver • Radio transmitter and receiver combined as one unit.

transponder • A transceiver that automatically sends a specified reply upon receipt of a specified signal.

UHF • Ultra high frequency, 300mHz–3000mHz.

useful load • Weight of fuel, occupants, survival gear, supplies, equipment and luggage; maximum gross weight cannot be exceeded when useful load is added to an aircraft's empty weight.

VFR • Visual flight rules optional for use when the cloud ceiling is higher than 1,000 feet and visibility is 3 miles or more.

VHF • Very high frequency, 30mHz–300mHz; used for normal aircraft voice communication and standard navigation.

VLF/Omega • A very low frequency (20kHz–30kHz) ground-based navigation system; susceptible to solar disturbances.

Volmet • A small number of radio stations around the world that continuously broadcast recorded meteorological conditions of a few major airports in a specific region; a pilot must be wary of their accuracy in remote locations.

VOR • VHF omnidirectional radio range, a short-range, ground-based navigational aid transmitting signals in all directions with magnetic north as a reference; sometimes called "omni."

Zulu time • The date and time at 000°00'00" longitude; use of "Z" time in international communications and travel achieves a worldwide common reference not possible with local times; time always uses the 24-hour clock of 0000 to 2359. Also called GMT [Greenwich Mean Time] or UTC [Universal Time Coordinated].

Index

ABOUT THE AUTHORS

Tom Towle, Jr., is president of a management and consulting firm based in Miami, Florida, and a certified real estate broker. A graduate of the Syracuse University Business School, Towle has more than 30 years' flying experience.

Fran Towle is a registered, licensed dietitian. A graduate of Rosary College (Illinois) and Florida International University, she has pursued a career in food service management and teaching.

The Towles have three school-aged children and live in the Miami area.